THE SOFA RULE

A BIBLICAL APPROACH TO GOD'S SOVEREIGNTY AND HUMAN RESPONSIBILITY

Christopher Cone Th.D, Ph.D, Ph.D

Exegetica Publishing
2019

"This is God's universe and He does things His way. You may have a better way, but you don't have a universe."

– J. Vernon McGee

For my Lovely Bride and our two Lovelies. *The Sofa Rule* is more precious to me because I am blessed to share the sofa with you.

For my co-laborers in preparing Christians to live and serve according to *the* Biblical worldview. Thank you for your faithfulness. May we strive diligently to walk in awe of Him.

The Sofa Rule: A Biblical Approach to God's Sovereignty and Human Responsibility

©2019 Christopher Cone

Published by Exegetica Publishing
Lee's Summit, Missouri

ISBN – 978-0-9982805-3-0

All rights reserved. No part of this publication may be reproduced, stored in a retrieval system, or transmitted in any form or by any means – electronic, mechanical, photocopy, recording, or any other – except for brief quotation in printed reviews, without the prior permission of the publisher.

All Scripture quotations, except those noted otherwise are from the New American Standard Bible, ©1960,1962,1963,1968,1971,1972,1973,1975, 1977, and 1995 by the Lockman Foundation.

Table of Contents

PART 1: BIBLICAL FOUNDATIONS
1. The Game is Afoot...1
2. Whom Shall We Trust?..5
3. The Condition for Unconditional Blessing.......................11
4. Whence Comes the Hardened Heart?...............................17
5. More Hardened Hearts 23
6. Decreed for a Decree...27
7. Bad Things Happen...31
8. He Sleeps During Storms...37
9. Born Broken, But for Glory..41
10. The Potter and His Clay...47
11. Hastening the Day, and Other Oddities.........................55

PART 2: THEOLOGICAL, PHILOSOPHICAL,
AND PRACTICAL IMPLICATIONS
12. The Intersection of Philosophy, Theology, and Worldview..61
13. The Beautiful Paradox..65
14. I Was Born That Way...71
15. Why I Am Not a Calvinist...or an Arminian..................97
16. Does Grace Extend to Everyone?..................................123
17. No Time for Salvation...137
18. The TULIPburger...145
19. The History of the Problem of Evil...............................151
20. Aesthetics and the Problem of Evil...............................185
21. Can God Really Know?...201
22. Breaking the Hinge...213
23. Is God a Jerk?...221
24. Decisions, Decisions: The Interplay Between Sovereignty and Freedom in Decision Making................................225
25. The Sofa Rule...231

PART 1:

BIBLICAL FOUNDATIONS

1
The Game is Afoot

For me it was a remarkable and memorable evening. I was in *the room*. It was the first day of the seminary's semester, and the first day of my teaching ministry at this particular school. I was an eager twenty-three-year-old ready to test drive my recently attained seminary degree and to begin corrupting the next generation of seminary students. So for the first time, I was allowed in *the room*. It was sacred ground from my perspective. Others might have thought of it simply as a faculty lounge, but it was more than that to me. It was known to most as "the gold room," named matter-of-factly for the aging furniture that accommodated its guests. But from my vantage point the room was golden for other reasons, namely due to the wisdom and character of the teachers that enjoyed it. In that room faculty would gather to pray and discuss the issues of the day before heading to class.

Initially, I sat there quietly and respectfully, recognizing that there were others who had far more to offer than I. But as a discussion developed it was centered on issues pertaining to the sovereignty of God and human accountability. I saw an opportunity and I just couldn't resist. "Did God predestine Adam to fail? I asked. The question punctuated the discussion, and there was a thoughtful lull. "That's a tough question…" responded more than one in the room. We discussed for a while, with no resolution – only an uncomfortable tension, as each person wrestled with the implications of every possible answer. After all were suitably stumped, we prayed, thanking God for how incredible He is, and off to class we went.

I will never forget that brief discussion in that room that evening, for it was in that moment that I found myself first dissatisfied with the proposed resolutions of the apparent paradox of God's sovereignty and concurrent human responsibility. The two most popular explanations (Calvinism and Arminianism) were unsatisfactory to my skeptical mind, and I thought there had to be a better understanding. Now, I am sure that many have drawn the same conclusions over the years, and I don't pretend to have anything unique to bring to the discussion, but those many years ago, I committed to seeking a *Biblical* resolution, rather than one grounded in historical theology or extra-biblical philosophy.

On the one hand, we have Paul telling us how unfathomable and unsearchable are the ways of God,[1] and on the other, he prays that believers will grow in their understanding, and that they will be receptive to the breadth, length, height, and depth of His incredible love.[2] In another context, we have Jesus telling the disciples plainly about His impending death and resurrection, yet they were not understanding what He was saying.[3] Later, Jesus challenged

---

[1] Romans 11:33.
[2] Ephesians 3:14-19.
[3] Luke 18:31-34.

other disciples with the reality that His death and resurrection had been revealed with clarity in earlier Scriptures.[4] Those things that the disciples had not understood about Him had not been understood because of our characteristic foolishness and slowness of heart to believe the word of God, and Jesus called them on it. Further, we are told that God's ways and thoughts are so much higher and beyond our own,[5] but in that same context we are told about the effectiveness and sufficiency of His word.[6] This tells us much about where we should search for truth.

In short, if eternal life is ultimately to know God,[7] and we have that life *right now*,[8] then our quest to learn and to know Him does not begin at heaven's door. It begins the moment we believe. At our new birth we begin a journey of learning and discovery – an adventure in which we can fathom any unfathomable things which His word has revealed. Our knowledge can extend as far as He has communicated, and we need not be lost in speculations and uncertainty when we can instead stand firmly and confidently in the truth that He has given us.

So, the game is afoot. Our grand adventure is to learn all we can of God from the eternal truth He has revealed. In our zeal for learning of Him, we must exercise caution only in not going beyond what is written.[9] We are given the creation to examine, and in it we discover many questions we ought to ask. Some answers lie within the creation itself. But many of the

---

[4] Luke 24:24-27.
[5] Isaiah 55:8-9.
[6] Isaiah 55:10-11.
[7] John 17:3.
[8] John 6:47.
[9] 1 Corinthians 4:6.

questions find their answers only in Scripture. So we must examine both the creation and His word tirelessly and humbly, eagerly receiving what we can know of our Lord, in His design. Our loving Father perhaps plays a bit of hide and seek with us, telling us we can find something of Him in creation,[10] and that we should search diligently to find more of Him in His word.[11] He has given of Himself freely and revealed Himself in such a way as to be understood. Of course, we have no means of knowing Him beyond the limits of His revelation, so we must be cautious about speculations that cannot lead to certainty. We cannot know (of Him) what He has not told us. But we can know what He has designed for us to know. Where the line is between the two is not our concern. Let us simply question and examine until the limits are exhausted.

  The game is afoot. Let's play it well! The prize is a greater and more certain knowledge of the One who loves us and knows us more than we could ever imagine. As you enjoy the game, I pray that Biblical resolutions to the apparent paradoxes will become evident to you. I believe they are resolutions communicated straightforwardly in Scripture and illustrated beautifully in many aspects of everyday life – even through a simple rule pertaining to a particular dark brown sofa – a sofa to which before this work is done, you will be introduced.

---

[10] Romans 1:20.
[11] E.g., 2 Timothy 2:15, John 5:39.

2
Whom Shall We Trust?

In any worldview there is a necessary first step of establishing the source of authority. Simply put, our first step is a step of faith in determining who or what we will trust in order to answer the questions of life. This is the first task of epistemology. For Hume that source of authority is human experience through the lens of the senses. Hume trusts the sensory abilities as the only trustworthy means of determining truth. Descartes, on the other hand, argues that the senses are less than reliable, and truth must be gathered through a process of reason guided by his method. For Descartes the human apparatus of reason can be harnessed in such a way as to lead us to truth. Nietzsche's model is less reliant on either the senses or reason, and instead trusts the self as the ultimate arbiter of truth. Plato saw limitations of both experience and reason, and considered enlightened learning a better way to come to a true knowledge of reality. His divided line theory provided a model seemingly advantageous to the philosopher in arriving at truth.

These first steps of faith suggested by Plato, Descartes, Hume, and Nietzsche have been broadly received, as they ground prominent worldviews. However, they do not account for the inherent limitations of learning, reason, experience, and perspective (the latter in Nietzsche's case). Consequently, while they each are broadly explanatory, they are not, in my estimation, satisfactorily explanatory in the quest for truth.

The Bible, on the other hand, makes sweeping claims regarding the source of authority. Solomonic epistemology, for example, is grounded on the premise that competing epistemic groundings are vanity.[1] The pursuit of wisdom and learning, while certainly having practical value, is ultimately futility and striving after wind[2] and even leads to grief and pain.[3] The stimulation of the senses, though temporally rewarding, is vanity, striving after wind, and unprofitable.[4] The pursuit of self is inherently limited,[5] cannot aid in what comes after this earthly life,[6] and ultimately is characterized more by evil and insanity than wellbeing and certainty.[7]

Solomon prescribes each of these terrestrial pursuits insofar as they have value, but only if the interlocutor is first willing to acknowledge that these pursuits are not ends in themselves. He advocates pursuing wisdom and learning, but only with the understanding that God will bring every resulting act to judgment.[8] Solomon advises the use of reason for its benefits,[9] but acknowledges that its use is limited in comparison

---

[1] Ecclesiastes 1:1.
[2] 2:12-17, 7:23-29.
[3] 1:12-18.
[4] 2:1-11.
[5] 3:11.
[6] 6:10-12.
[7] 9:3.
[8] 12:9-13.
[9] 10:10

to the certainties God possesses.[10] Solomon encourages the stimulation of the senses, but only insofar as they are used in the context of remembering the Creator, because those senses will become increasingly ineffective until ultimately they are silenced in death.[11] Finally, Solomon advocates following the impulses of the heart (the self), but only with the admission that God will judge the follower for those pursuits.[12]

Solomon answers each epistemological model with the same alternative: a beyond-the-sun worldview provides certainty, whereas an under-the-sun worldview provides none. Simply put, under the sun we do not know the activity of God who makes all things.[13] Consequently, for us to have a worldview grounded in certainty, it must be premised on an acknowledgement of the Creator. Solomon pronounces that records of truth – wisdom and delightful words – are given by one Shepherd,[14] and in so stating reveals that God's word is the answer to the epistemological first inquiry regarding what is the source of authority. Elsewhere, Solomon recognizes that the fear of the Lord is the beginning of knowledge,[15] the beginning of wisdom, and that the knowledge of the Holy One is understanding.[16]

Solomon writes so that his readers will know wisdom and instruction and have discernment,[17] to instruct them in the fear

---

[10] 11:5.
[11] 12:1-8.
[12] 11:9-10.
[13] 11:5.
[14] 12:9-11.
[15] Proverbs 1:7.
[16] 9:10.
[17] 1:1.

of the Lord as the source of strong confidence and refuge.[18] Consequently he prescribes that humanity must fear God.[19] And what is the authoritative source from whence we discover the fear of the Lord? Solomon answers this all-important question directly: "Then you will discern the fear of the Lord, and discover the knowledge of God. For the Lord gives wisdom; from His mouth come knowledge and understanding.[20] God's word, according to Solomon, is the source of authority whereby we can have certainty.

Consequently, theological conclusions can only be as certain as they are revealed in Scripture. Once we move beyond what is written, we are engaging in extra-biblical speculations, and in those contexts one's guess is not better than that of another. To resolve questions and paradoxes as challenging as those offered by Calvinism, Arminianism, and the problem of evil, let's examine what the Bible actually says, and be alert for doctrines that go beyond what is written. Paul reminds his readers in 1 Corinthians 4:6 that they should learn not to go beyond what is written so that they will not become arrogant towards one another. And indeed, that warning proves applicable, especially in the context of resolving challenging theological questions.

These are not merely theoretical or conceptual questions. It is not as if they have no real bearing on core elements of life. If we don't answer these issues well, then we will fail to understand who God is, who we are, what we are designed to be, and how He intends for us to grow and to walk. These are significant considerations, and we must address them in a way

---

[18] 14:26.
[19] Ecclesiastes 3:14, 5:7, 12:13.
[20] Proverbs 2:5-6.

that provides certain conclusions. God is our Source of authority, and He has revealed Himself in Scripture. Let's examine what *He* has said and see if we can avoid speculations and uncertainties.

10   The Sofa Rule

3

The Condition for Unconditional Blessing

The Abrahamic Covenant, first iterated in Genesis 12:1-3 and later detailed in Genesis 15-17, is usually understood to be unconditional. Once it is pronounced by God and then ratified, it is set in motion and the promised outcomes are certain. In that sense, once the covenant was actually *cut,* it was unconditional. Still it is worth noting that the catalog of promises set forth in 12:2-3 is preceded by instructions that Abram was to follow God on a journey. In this sense, the covenant was preceded by a condition that needed to be met in order for the covenant to be enacted. While God is expressing His sovereignty in making commitments that obligated Him to future action, He also is requiring of Abram a degree of responsibility upon which God's commitment (at least initially) would rest. In this way the Abrahamic Covenant provides a valuable case study for our understanding of how God perceives His own sovereignty, human responsibility, and how those two seemingly paradoxical concepts interact.

12 The Sofa Rule

There are several notable conditional statements given in the early Genesis narrative. The first is in Genesis 2:17: "from the tree of the knowledge of good and evil you shall not eat (qal imperfect), for in the day you eat of it, to die (qal infinitive) you will die (qal imperfect)." This statement was a warning of associated conditions, and God viewed the warning as a direct command[1] – in order for one condition (death) to be avoided, the other condition (forbidden eating) must also be avoided. Once the first condition became reality, the second did as well. As Romans 5:12-21 explains, death came to all through one transgression. (Thankfully, this explanation doesn't leave us in that condition without a revealed remedy.)

An ontological shift is evident from the conclusion of the creation week, at which point all of creation is described as very good (*tov meod*),[2] and the period of Noah's generation, in which "the wickedness of man was great (*rabbah*) on the earth."[3] The result was a change of mind on God's part[4] – an axiological assessment on God's part that an ontological change had occurred within His creation. The ontological change was profound, to the point that God was *emotionally* impacted[5] and moved to action.[6]

We see a similar series of events in God's dealings with Abraham, in Genesis 12 and following. God selects Abraham without revealing the reason for His choice. He tells Abram (so named at the time) to go,[7] and then adds a series of seven

---

[1] Genesis 3:11.
[2] 1:31.
[3] 6:5.
[4] 6:6-7.
[5] 6:7.
[6] 6:8.
[7] 12:1.

promises that God would fulfill.[8] Without reading on to verse 4 (yet), we can stop and consider whether or not God was already obligated at the point of pronouncement. If He had already obligated Himself, then Abram's obedience was irrelevant (at least in relation to the promises' fulfillments). If God was not yet obligated, then perhaps Abram's obedience would provide a necessary condition for blessing. If we choose the former, and conclude that God was not yet obligated, then we might be favorable to a Calvinist approach, concluding that human choice is irrelevant. On the other hand, if we choose the latter, then we might be sympathetic to an Arminian approach, which looks completely to human response in order to direct God's response.

Though God is the Creator, and though He has thus far expressed sovereignty over His creation, the Biblical data shows that sovereignty does not preclude ontological changes within His creation that would cause Him to make axiological reassessments and have emotional responses. As they seek to explain how such responses are possible, the Calvinist and Arminian paradigms, respectively, suggest that God is either without (passively derived) passions altogether,[9] or that his passions can only be aroused by a change in experiential knowledge. But the Biblical data seems to imply there is a third option.

It is notable, then, that while 12:4 tells us that Abram went as God had instructed him, there is no contextual discussion of the hypotheticals. There are only statements of reality as it unfolds. Even at this point, there is an implication of a third approach – an alternative to the apparent paradox that

---

[8] 12:2-3.
[9] *Westminster Confession of Faith*, 2.1.

the Calvinist and Arminian understandings infer. That third approach becomes more apparent as the narrative continues.

Genesis 15 records the restatement and actual cutting of the covenant God made with Abraham.[10] God puts Abraham to sleep, and only God "signs" the deal. In that sense the covenant is unilateral, and at that point it would seem an appropriate assumption that Abraham's actions moving forward would not be relevant to the fulfilling of the covenant promises. Yet in Genesis 22:16-18, during events taking place years after the covenant's ratification, several of the covenant blessings are restated, and God says He will do them, "because you have obeyed My voice." The NASB translation of *esher* in 22:16 and 22:18 is *because,* and denotes a causative relationship of obedience to blessing. However, the term can also be used in a comparative sense, as is the case in Genesis 41:28, "It is as I have spoken to Pharaoh..." Also, the complementing *eqeb* of 22:18 (which together with *esher* form the phrase translated by the NASB as *because*) can also refer to a state of completion – *the end* – as in Psalm 119:33, "Teach me Your statutes, O Lord, and I shall observe it *to the end.*" With these two considerations in view, Genesis 22:16 could be translated, "as you have done this thing and not withheld your son..." and 22:18 could read, "In your seed all the nations of the earth will be blessed *to the end* just as you have obeyed My voice."

In this understanding, God would be illustrating His own faithfulness at all costs through Abraham's willing obedience, allowing Abraham to see just how committed God was to keeping His word. This would have been a very personal and powerful lesson for Abraham, and not one soon forgotten. In this

---

[10] 15:18.

understanding, Abraham's action did not determine God's course of action, but nor was it irrelevant. There was a third option in view: God's sovereignty would be unaffected by human responsibility, but God still demanded human responsibility – in this case, to help Abraham *experience* the commitment level of God. God's sovereignty and human responsibility work hand in hand in the achieving of and illustrating of God's purposes.

16 The Sofa Rule

4
Whence Comes The Hardened Heart?

Moses is frustrated. He had been rebuffed by Pharaoh, and now his fellow Israelites were experiencing severe consequences. Moses questions God, wondering how only harm has come to Israel since God sent him.[1] God responds, telling Moses that He will act upon Pharaoh, compelling him to let Israel go, and to drive them from Egypt.[2] In the first nine verses of Exodus 6 God uses eight "I will" verbs indicating the actions He would take, to: (1) do something to Pharaoh so he would act under compulsion, (2) bring Israel out, (3) deliver Israel from bondage, (4) redeem Israel, (5) take Israel for His people, (6) be their God, (7) bring them to the promised land, and (8) give that land to Israel as a possession.

As if those eight verbs were not clear enough, God emphasizes again what He would do and why: "I will harden Pharaoh's heart that I may multiply My signs and My wonders

---

[1] Exodus 5:2-23.
[2] 6:1.

in the land of Egypt."[3] God preannounces that Pharaoh would not listen to Moses, and when that took place, God would bring Israel out of Egypt and judge the people of Egypt.[4]

After the first sign (Aaron's staff becoming a serpent and swallowed up the staves of the Egyptian magi) Pharaoh's heart strengthened or grew strong, and Pharaoh did not listen to Moses and Aaron, just as God had told them.[5] The same phrasing is used to describe Pharaoh after the second sign – the waters turned to blood.[6] After the infestation of frogs in the third sign, Pharaoh's heart was caused to be hardened or heavy – again, just as God had said.[7] The fourth sign brought a plague of lice, and Pharaoh's heart strengthened again (just as in 7:13 and 22).

The fifth sign was swarms of flies, and this time Pharaoh caused his own heart to be hardened.[8] The hifil stem in Hebrew shows causative action in the active voice, and in 8:15, and 8:32 the hifil is used. In these instances, Pharaoh's heart is causing itself to strengthen, and Pharaoh causes his heart to strengthen. Sixth, many of the livestock throughout Egypt died. Just as in previous instances, Pharaoh's heart strengthened.[9] The seventh sign was a severe plague of boils that affected humans and animals alike. In this case, God severely hardened the heart of Pharaoh.[10] In this instance, the use of the piel stem in Hebrew shows intensity – God actively and severely hardened the heart

---

[3] 7:3.
[4] 7:4-5.
[5] 7:13.
[6] 7:22.
[7] 8:15.
[8] 8:32.
[9] 9:7.
[10] 9:12.

of Pharaoh. The eighth sign was the most severe plague of hail the nation had ever seen. At first, Pharaoh was repentant,[11] but he sinned again and caused[12] his heart to be strengthened.[13]

The ninth sign was a plague of locusts more severe than the nation had experienced or ever would.[14] Again, Pharaoh was briefly repentant, but again, his heart was hardened. This time, it was God who strengthened Pharaoh's heart.[15] A tenth sign was three days of darkness over the whole land of Egypt. Again, God strengthened Pharaoh's heart.[16]

The eleventh sign, and the tenth plague,[17] was the death of the firstborn throughout Egypt. In 11:9-10 we read an interlude reminding that God had preannounced all this to Moses, that Pharaoh would not listen, and that God would strengthen Pharaoh's heart so that he would not allow the people of Israel to leave. This passage also reminds us of the reason: that God's signs or wonders would be multiplied in Egypt. Now that God's signs had been multiplied, Pharaoh finally allowed the Israelites to leave Egypt. Yet even in this, God had foretold that Pharaoh would ultimately change his mind, as God would again strengthen the heart of Pharaoh[18] – God would be honored through Pharaoh and his army, and the Egyptians would know that God was Yahweh.[19]

---

[11] 9:27-28.
[12] Another instance of the hifil stem.
[13] 9:35.
[14] 10:14-15.
[15] 10:20, piel intensive stem.
[16] 10:27, piel intensive stem.
[17] The first sign – Aaron's rod budding was a sign, but not a plague.
[18] 14:4, piel intensive stem.
[19] 14:4.

After the deliverance of Israel from Egypt, the people sang a song of praise to God, and the concluding words of the song were, "Yahweh shall be King forever."[20] Miriam added that God had hurled the horse and rider into the sea.[21] Moses, Miriam, and all those singing recognized that God was in control all along. In all this He was simply exercising His sovereign rights as King of all, in order to accomplish His purposes. His name was magnified, and now both the sons of Israel and the people of Egypt knew who He was.

It is especially noteworthy that while God preannounced that He would strengthen or harden Pharaoh's heart – and did so – Pharaoh also *caused his own heart to be hardened*. These events show us that God is sovereign, and people are accountable. These two concepts are not contradictory, and we don't need to pretend that somehow free will is necessary for God to hold someone accountable. While we cannot say that Pharaoh's will was *free*, we can certainly say that he exercised his volition, and that God held him accountable. But ultimately, it was God who was in control.

While some might question God's methods, those critics don't have a fraction of the perspective and understanding that God has. As J.V. McGee once famously said, "This is God's universe and He does things His way. You may have a better way, but you don't have a universe." Don't like how God is sovereign and still holds people accountable? Get your own universe. And that is exactly how Romans 1 describes those who reject God – they reject His design and try to redefine reality in such a way as to liberate them from being subject to His sovereignty. Not only is that a nonsensical enterprise, but it also

---

[20] 15:18.
[21] 15:21.

causes them to miss what an incredibly gracious and compassionate Sovereign He is.[22]

---

[22] 33:19.

22 The Sofa Rule

5
More Hardened Hearts

For the moment the Israelites were rejoicing. They had been delivered from centuries of slavery and were now on their way to a land God would give them. They began their journey with boldness,[1] and the future looked bright. The first leg of the journey had been completed, and they were setting up camp not far from the shore.[2] But they apparently hadn't yet realized that the journey would not be without obstacles, and there was one major hurdle that had to be cleared. Pharaoh was drawing near, and the Egyptians with him.[3] When the Israelites realized they were being pursued they were very afraid. They were beginning to realize that they had nowhere to go – there was a body of water in front of them, and an army of Egyptians behind them.

While their first move was to cry out to the Lord, it doesn't appear they were crying out expecting Him to deliver them, as their next move was to question Moses, thinking he had brought

---

[1] Exodus 14:8.
[2] 14:9.
[3] 14:10.

them to a place where they would all be killed.[4] They began to think fondly of their enslavement, as if it was better than their imminent deaths. At the hands of the Egyptian warriors.[5]

Moses exhibits great leadership, assuring the people that God would deliver them in a mighty way.[6] In this courageous moment, we see a practical importance of understanding God's sovereignty and human responsibility. Recall how God had worked with Moses earlier in Exodus, explaining to Moses how God would impact Pharaoh's heart and what the outcome would be. Moses saw God's word fulfilled, and now at the precipice of destruction, Moses was able to stand firm in trusting God. *Understanding who God is and how He works gives us courage to meet any task He has placed before us.*

God's next move is a bit humorous: He challenges Moses that the time for talking is done. It is now time to act. Israel should move forward, and God would have Moses divide the waters of the sea so that Israel can cross on dry land.[7] It is important to note that not only does God tell Moses what Israel's part and Moses' part would be in this great deliverance, but He also explains what *He would do*. God would harden the hearts of Pharaoh *and his army* so that they would attempt to cross the sea in pursuit of the Israelites. Through this God would make Himself known among all the Egyptian people – again His glory is in view.[8]

In this historic moment of salvation for the nation of Israel, we do not simply see the sovereignty of God *or* the

---

[4] 14:11.
[5] 14:12.
[6] 14:13-14.
[7] 14:15-16.
[8] 14:17-18.

responsibility of humanity. We see both. In fact, notice that there are several pieces in play here: (1) God is sovereignly impacting hearts and manipulating nature, (2) Moses has to take leadership, (3) the Israelites have to move forward trusting that God would deliver them, and (4) the Egyptian Pharaoh and army would be instruments to demonstrate God's glory. God designed these events in such a way that four parties had to do their part. God is sovereign and humanity is responsible.

Once Moses had learned that lesson, he could lead well and act with courage. Once Israel learned to trust in Him *and understand their responsibility*, they could move forward. Through the (tragic) deaths of the Egyptians Pharaoh and army, the nation of Egypt was introduced yet again to the greatness of God. In all of this God is demonstrating His sovereignty and His character – and He did it by involving people and by making them accountable. This wasn't the first time He would harden hearts and it would not be the last.

Now, it may seem unsavory that God would harden hearts – especially in such a way that would lead to the deaths of those whose hearts were hardened. There are two things to consider here. First, recall J.V. McGee's comment that "This is God's universe and He does things His way. You may have a better way, but you don't have a universe." He has the prerogative to do things like this, whether you and I like it or not. He is the Creator – all that exists is His to do with as He sees best. Second, we must understand that His perspective is so much more accurate than ours. For example, all we know is this brief lifetime, and when we think about a lifetime being ended in death, we can't think of a more traumatic and final event. But God recognizes that death – while never a good thing, because it is part of the curse of sin[9] – God has a plan to overcome it. That first death is *temporary* and He has overcome it.[10] In fact, in Psalm 116:15 we are even told that the death of His godly ones is *precious* to Him. Why? We can't fathom that. It doesn't fit our limited perspective of being all-in on this earthly life. Clearly, He knows something that we don't. And in a number of passages He helps us have a glimpse of what He is thinking. Still, sometimes He doesn't give us more information. He doesn't fill in those gaps. We simply have to make a choice: will we trust Him or not?

---

[9] Genesis 3.
[10] 1 Corinthians 15:53-57.

6
Decreed for a Decree

Daniel 9:24-27 is a monumental passage, emblematic of God's sovereignty over human events. It provides the chronological skeletal system of Biblical prophecy, recording Gabriel's revelation to Daniel in around 516 B.C., of a 490-year timeline for Israel's future: "for Jerusalem, to make an end of sin, to make atonement for iniquity, to bring in everlasting righteousness, to seal up vision and prophecy, and to anoint the most holy."[1] The clock begins its countdown with "a decree to restore and rebuild Jerusalem."[2]

The certainty of the timeline is non-negotiable and inalterable. The seventy sevens had been decreed or determined, as the Hebrew term *nichetaka* (*decreed, determined*) is in the niphal perfect, which typically indicates a passive (niphal) and completed (perfect) action. The timeline had *already* been determined. Daniel would be able to "know and discern"[3] the

---

[1] Daniel 9:24.
[2] 9:25.
[3] 9:25a.

timing from a particular point in history – a decree to restore and rebuild Jerusalem.

When we examine the Biblical literature, we find only one decree regarding the rebuilding of the temple. There was a decree to rebuild the temple,[4] but that did not match Gabriel's description of the decree to rebuild the city itself. For the decree matching the Daniel 9 description, we look to Nehemiah 2.

When we are first introduced to Nehemiah, we find him praying in a similar fashion to Daniel's prayer. Nehemiah weeps for his people and his city,[5] acknowledges the faithfulness of God in keeping His word,[6] confesses not only the sin of his people, but also his own sin and that of his father's house,[7] and he appeals to God to remember His word and the promises He made to Israel.[8] After recording the prayer, Nehemiah makes a point to tell the readers that he was cupbearer to the king.[9] This is significant, for his readers would understand that he had a high degree of responsibility, not only in being the official taste-tester to protect the king from danger, but also as an administrator, possibly keeping the signet and in charge of high levels of administration, as in the apocryphal reference to Ahiqar of the Assyrian court.[10]

Josephus records that Nehemiah was outside the palace at a gate inquiring of the welfare of Jews who had returned to Jerusalem, Nehemiah was told that they were being overrun, and that there were even corpses in the roads. While Nehemiah

---

[4] Ezra 1:1-4, 5:17.
[5] Nehemiah 1:4.
[6] 1:5.
[7] 1:6-7.
[8] 1:8-11.
[9] 1:11.
[10] Tobit 1:22.

was grieving there at the gate, he was told that the king was about to dine. Nehemiah hurried back, "as he was, without even washing" to serve the king.[11]

If Josephus' account reflects accurately, it is no wonder that Nehemiah was afraid,[12] as he had not been previously troubled before the king, nor was it likely he had previously appeared so unready to dispense with his duty. Nehemiah's fear, then, was justified, as his life was at stake. When asked why he appeared so troubled, Nehemiah offered no apology, but respectfully recounted how the city of Jerusalem remained in ruins.[13] The king responded favorably, inviting Nehemiah to make a request. Before he responded to the king, Nehemiah prayed.[14] Nehemiah then requested of the king that he be allowed to return to Jerusalem and rebuild the city.[15] The king granted his request and sent with Nehemiah royal letters confirming his decree that Nehemiah was to rebuild the city. Nehemiah recognized that the king's cooperation was attributed to God's favor.[16]

Without Nehemiah's prayerful response to the king and his passion for Jerusalem it seems this decree doesn't happen, yet the timeline itself had already been decreed long before Nehemiah. In this episode Nehemiah demonstrated patriotism, courage, humility, and above all dependence on his Lord. As a result of Nehemiah's response, King Artaxerxes' decree of 445-444 B.C. would quietly yet significantly set in motion the Daniel 9 timeline. God had already decreed the timeline, and at the

---

[11] Josephus, *Antiquities*, 11:1:159-163.
[12] Nehemiah 2:1-2.
[13] 2:3.
[14] 2:4.
[15] 2:5.
[16] 2:8.

same time he uses and responds to Nehemiah. In this case it is evident that God is both completely sovereign, and that humanity bears responsibility for and shares at least some degree of involvement in the unfolding of God's plan.

7
Bad Things Happen

You recall how the story goes – God and Satan are having a discussion about a man named Job. He was a man of great character whom God had given much wealth and blessing. God commends Job, and Satan accuses Job, betting that Job would deny God if God would simply allow difficulty in Job's life.[1] God allows Satan to test Job, and Job loses all of his wealth, most of his family, and his health. Job is, of course, unaware that he is being tested, and is deeply frustrated by his change of fortune.

He feels that he has done nothing to deserve these tragedies, and he speaks out – essentially proclaiming his innocence and the unfairness of the situation. Thankfully, Job has three friends who come to the rescue. They all have the same message: this could only be happening to Job if he had done something wrong. They understood that God would not allow such things to happen to an innocent person. Here's a brief summary of Job 3-31:

---

[1] Job 1:7-12.

> Job: I didn't do anything to deserve this.
> Friends: Yes you did.
> Job: No I didn't.
> Friends: Yes you did.
> Job: No I didn't.
> Friends: Yes you did. God wouldn't allow it otherwise.
> Job: This isn't fair…because I didn't do anything wrong.

Now, I don't mean to make light of Job's situation – it was one of the most severe individual tragedies ever recorded, and I believe he was a real person who underwent intense pain and suffering. I think we can read the dialogues of Job and his "friends" with empathy while still being able to distill the discussions down to their most basic concepts. As we read, we discover that God's character is the primary issue, along with the question of why God allows evil things to happen to people. Chapters 3-31 invite the big questions but provide no answers.

Finally, in chapter 32, we are introduced to a young man who has been sitting by and listening in silence, waiting for Job's three friends to respond well. Elihu recognizes that Job and his friends have made some key mistakes: Job had justified himself before God,[2] and the three friends had condemned Job without being able to refute him.[3]

In chapter 33 Elihu challenges Job's assertion that God does not explain why He is doing what He is doing.[4] Elihu argues that God has revealed himself in many ways. Now, remember that Job was written around the time of the events in Genesis, so Job and his contemporaries did not yet have any written

---

[2] 32:3.
[3] 32:4.
[4] 33:13.

revelation from God. Even then, God communicated with people to protect, correct, and enlighten them.[5] God was gracious even then.

Elihu then addresses Job's friends.[6] They had argued that God could not allow such misfortune to befall Job without guilt being involved. Little did they realize that they were accusing God of unrighteousness and injustice, because Job had no guilt in the situation (in all this Job did not sin with his lips[7]). Elihu recognizes that God is righteous and just,[8] but also that God is sovereign over His creation (as its Creator) and has the right to do with it as He determines.[9]

I should note at this point that some commentators have perceived that Elihu to be equally as wrongheaded as Job's other three friends, because those commentators suspect that Elihu is condemning Job of sin. But it is important to recognize that Elihu never accuses Job of sin. He recognizes that the "wise men" and "men of understanding" have accused Job of sin and rebellion,[10] but he never agrees with them. Instead, Elihu accuses Job of speaking in ignorance,[11] which is a very different accusation altogether. Further, at the end of the book God rebukes Job[12] and the three friends,[13] but never Elihu. Ultimately God's words and those of Elihu are rooted in the same basic argument (that God is Creator, and as such is

---

[5] 33:16-18, 29-30.
[6] 34.
[7] 2:10.
[8] 34:1-12.
[9] 34:13-15.
[10] 34:34-37.
[11] 35:16.
[12] 38-41.
[13] 42:7.

sovereign over His creation) and are at times even indistinguishable. Elihu gets it right. Job acknowledges his own ignorance,[14] and the three are guilty of misrepresenting Job and God.

Elihu understands that God has his own reasons for causing things to happen. Sometimes these reasons are indiscernible to us, but they are good reasons nonetheless: "Whether for correction, or for His world, or for lovingkindness, He causes it to happen."[15] Elihu offers three reasons for God's activity, suggesting that we can trust God to know what He is doing, and to be beneficial to His creation *according to His own designs*. The problem is that we expect Him to work in ways *we* can comprehend. Yet, just as we cannot comprehend all the inner workings of the natural world like He does, we sometimes cannot comprehend what He is doing and why. Just as scientific study helps us to gain some understanding of the natural world, study of God's revelation helps us understand His character better. The more we grow in that understanding, the more likely we are to be able to comprehend at least the big picture of what God is doing. In any case, Elihu is confident in God, trusting Him to know and to do what is best for His creation.

Elihu gets it right, and offers encouraging advice to anyone struggling with incomprehensible difficulties in life. God is sovereign, He understands, and He has a plan. He is all-powerful, all-knowing, and all-beneficent. As Creator, His plans are a bit better constructed than our own.[16] Because of that He

---

[14] 42:1-6.
[15] 37:13.
[16] Isaiah 55:8-11.

is worthy of praise.[17] Do we really think that we know better than God? Do we really think that we have a right to condemn Him when things don't go as we expect they should? Or are we willing to trust that He has things under control, and in the end, the wrongs will be righted? Even in Job 42 we see the narrative resolved. Surely we can have a little patience with God. He certainly has great patience with us.[18]

---

[17] Romans 11:33-36.
[18] 2 Peter 3:9.

36 The Sofa Rule

8
He Sleeps During Storms

They were paralyzed with fear. The waves were crashing over the boat, and it could capsize at any moment. They could see it coming. The only thing standing between them and certain death was...well, *nothing*. It was just a matter of time. Imagine their surprise when they realized that Jesus was not panicking with them. He lay calmly in the storm-tossed boat, *asleep*. Where is God when I need Him? Why is He not taking action? Why is He not delivering me from this hardship? Jesus was about to teach the disciples how to handle these questions, and He would start by sleeping.

Not long before that, Jesus was teaching on the shore, challenging his disciples about the cost of following Him.[1] Perhaps now as their demise seemed imminent, they may have wondered if the cost was too high. What if they hadn't followed Him – what if they hadn't followed His directive to cross the sea right then?[2] Surely worsening weather conditions made it fairly obvious that traveling by boat was a fool's errand. They woke

---
[1] Matthew 8:18-28.
[2] 8:18.

Him up, showing a mustard seed of faith – "Save us Lord, we are perishing!"[3] This simple request showed how highly they thought of Him. They believed He could save them from *nature*. I am guessing they hadn't thought of exactly how He might save them, but their childlike faith in Him was at least evident. Jesus awoke, and challenged them to have greater faith – "Why are you afraid, men of little faith?"[4] These men had been with Jesus. They had seen His miracles, and they had heard His teaching, yet still they had only a small faith.

Perhaps it could be said that the smaller the faith, the greater the fear, and the greater the faith demonstrated, the lesser the fear. In this case, Jesus allowed their lives to be threatened in order for them to be confronted with the reality that they simply needed to trust Him more. Once He established that, He demonstrated His sovereignty over nature, something that only the Creator could accomplish: He governed the weather and the sea, and they obeyed Him immediately, as a great calm occurred. The disciples responded in amazement. They had trusted in Him, but not to the extent that He wanted. Now they were beginning to recognize that He was indeed sovereign. They asked, "who is this man that even the winds and the sea obey Him?"[5]

This episode confronts us with the reality that sometimes God works this way – sometimes He is working to accomplish the testing, stretching, and strengthening of our trust in Him, and sometimes that process means we are hit with circumstances we cannot understand. We can respond in fear, or we can respond in faith, but the two don't go together. Just as

---

[3] 8:25.
[4] 8:26.
[5] 8:27.

perfect love casts out fear,[6] He allows us to encounter fearful situations that we cannot otherwise contextualize outside of simply exercising faith in Him. His love is working to cast out our fear, and He does it by building our faith in Him.

When things seem out of control, they aren't. Perhaps He is simply allowing us to go through the process so we can learn that lesson. If He is willing to take a nap in the most adverse of conditions, then we can trust Him and we can rest in Him during even the greatest of difficulties.

---

[6] 1 John 4:18.

40   The Sofa Rule

9

Born Broken, But for Glory

One of the most fascinating stories in the entire Bible is found in John 9. There was a man who was born blind. As Jesus was passing by with His disciples, seeing this poor, underprivileged man, they asked Jesus, "who sinned, this man or his parents that he would be born blind?"[1] The disciples were thinking like Job's three friends, that personal calamity was a direct result of sin. These disciples just weren't sure whose sin was to blame. It seemed like a reasonable enough question, with two potential solutions that the disciples could live with. Either way, they could establish the purpose for such a sad state. They needed it explained. The tension of unresolved tragedy was for them – as it often is for us – too upsetting. So, they assumed the answer was one of two possibilities.

On the one hand, if the parents had sinned and the blindness was a consequence of their actions, that would square with the idea of generational judgment. After all, it had been

---

[1] John 9:2.

said that "the fathers eat the sour grapes and the children's teeth are set on edge."[2] Even the consequences of the first sin were felt by following generations, as they would eat of bread by their toil.[3] The disciples' understanding of the metaphysical realities of how a cursed creation operated was not far off, thus if the man's blindness was due to his parents' sin, the disciples probably would not have given it a second thought.

On the other hand, the disciples wondered if the man had himself somehow sinned before birth. In this scenario, the man's blindness was earned by his own action, even while in the womb. But how could that be? How could someone sin before even being born? Job had once recognized that God was actively forming the unborn,[4] as did David.[5] Jeremiah recounted the words of God, that before God had formed Jeremiah in the womb He had known him.[6] While David also had acknowledged that even coming from the womb humanity is active in wickedness,[7] there was no Biblical precedent for humanity *actually committing sin* in the womb. Sure, Jacob was said to have grabbed his brother's heel while in the womb,[8] but it was not said that there was sinfulness in that action.

The disciples had no Biblical data to point them to sin in the womb, but it certainly would have been *just* for the man to have been born blind if he had indeed sinned pre-birth. Surely, they were aware of the universality of the consequences of sin, and perhaps even the reality that, as David recognized,

---

[2] Jeremiah 31:29.
[3] Genesis 3:15-17.
[4] Job 31:15.
[5] Psalm 139:13.
[6] Jeremiah 1:5.
[7] Psalm 58:3.
[8] Genesis 25:26, Hosea 12:3.

humanity was conceived in sin.⁹ If the reason for the man's blindness was attributed directly to his own sin, then there would be no theological problem for the disciples. Their question seems a mere curiosity, as the two options they offered presented no real challenge to their understanding of how things worked. But Jesus was going to offer them a whole new paradigm. They were thinking like Job's three friends before Elihu and then God afterward corrected Job and the three. Jesus' response to the disciples' question offered a parallel to what we discover in the latter portions of the Book of Job: "Neither this man sinned, nor his parents, but [this was] so that the works of God might be displayed in him."¹⁰

This particular physical malady was not a direct consequence of sin. Jesus explained its purpose as displaying the works of God. *This man was born blind so that at that moment, Jesus could restore his sight!* Let that sink in for a moment. This man was a beggar on the streets, incapable of caring for himself because he couldn't see. He had endured a lifetime of suffering because eyesight was kept from him. And by whom was it kept from him? *By his Creator!* In this is a mystery unveiled. From the man's limited perspective, there was no way that moment could have been worth a lifetime of hardship, but from God's perspective, something so magnificent would be accomplished in that moment, that it would indeed be worth the cost to the man: "Since the beginning of time it has never been heard that anyone opened the eyes of a person born blind. If this man were not from God, He could do nothing.¹¹

---

⁹ Psalm 51:5.
¹⁰ John 9:3.
¹¹ 9:32-33.

In that moment, the deity of Jesus was demonstrated powerfully. God opens the eyes of the blind.[12] The Messiah would bring sight to those who could not see.[13] Jesus was the Messiah. Jesus was God.

In God's unlimited perspective He understands that a few decades are merely a speck in the life of a person that He has designed to live eternally. We focus so often with limited perspective on these brief years on earth as if they are everything, when they are really very insignificant when compared to eternity. What might appear cruel when viewed through a temporal lens can be seen to be incredibly gracious when perceived in the right context. Consider for a moment the perspective of a child who sees his parent allowing a doctor to pierce the child's arm with a needle. In that moment, the child may be terrified, hurt, and even angry at what appears to be a life-shaking betrayal. The parent who is tasked with loving and protecting that child is allowing someone to cause pain with a sharp object to their helpless child. In that moment, if the child sees only with that temporal perspective, then the moment is not at all worthwhile. However, what the child may be able to understand if they are well prepared is that the parent loves them, and is allowing them to receive medication that will help their body recover from a life threatening illness. A brief moment of anxiety, discomfort, and even pain is a miniscule price to pay for the cure that is being administered. If the child can see with those eyes, then not only is the momentary pain worth it, but perhaps their love and faith in the parent is even strengthened. What might have appeared at first as a betrayal was actually a great kindness.

---

[12] Psalm 146:8.
[13] Isaiah 35:5.

After this man was given sight, because he would not deny the One who restored his sight, he was cast out of the synagogue. He had undergone a lifetime of hardship and suffering, and now insult was added to injury. If he would have viewed life from a temporal vantage point, he certainly could have been embittered. Imagine learning that your hardship was for *show-and-tell*, imagine how frustrated you might become. But this man's response was not that at all. He didn't deny the Lord who had healed him, and then when Jesus approached him afterward, encouraging him to believe in Jesus, the man responded by saying, "Lord I believe," and he worshipped Jesus[14] – another evidence of Jesus' deity, by the way, that Jesus accepted his worship. This episode illustrates so powerfully the sovereignty and omniscience of God, and shows how He is gracious and kind, having the big picture in view. When we encounter difficulties that hurt or make us angry, we can respond ignorantly as if we are betrayed children, or we can respond like this man – with faith and with worship.

---

[14] John 9:35-38.

46 The Sofa Rule

10
The Potter and His Clay

"Jacob I loved, but Esau I hated."[1] Spurgeon referred to this statement as "a terrible text,"[2] and "an ugly text."[3] Indeed, these are jarring words. We like to think of God simply as love, because after all, John tells us that "God is love."[4] It would seem impossible that someone who is described as love could actually *hate* anyone. To understand what is happening here, we need some context.

First, we need to keep in mind that God's character is not *only* defined by love. Yes, God is love, but God is not only love. He is also just,[5] righteous,[6] retributive,[7] angry,[8] merciful,[9]

---

[1] Romans 9:13.
[2] C.H. Spurgeon, "Sermon Number 239," 1859, viewed at https://www.blueletterbible.org/Comm/spurgeon_charles/sermons/0239.cfm.
[3] Ibid.
[4] 1 John 4:8.
[5] Deuteronomy 32:4.
[6] Isaiah 45:21.
[7] Deuteronomy 32:35.
[8] Psalm 60:1.
[9] Psalm 86:15.

disciplinary,[10] jealous,[11] and a myriad of other things. But the characterization of God that He seems to prefer above all else is that He is *holy*.

In Isaiah 6:3 we come face to face with seraphim, one calling out to another, "Holy, Holy, Holy is the Lord of hosts, the whole earth is full of His glory." Then again in Revelation 4:8 we meet four creatures who unceasingly proclaim, "Holy, Holy, Holy is the Lord God Almighty, who was and who is and is to come." In each of these episodes, those beings closest to God identify Him with this thrice emphasized attribution of holiness. He accepts that worship and allows it to be revealed and heard. It is evident that the individual aspects of His revealed character are expressions of His holiness – His being entirely other, His separateness from His creation. Perhaps one of the best statements of what His holiness means, practically speaking is found in Isaiah 55:8-9,

> For My thoughts are not your thoughts, Nor are your ways My ways," declares the LORD. For *as* the heavens are higher than the earth, So are My ways higher than your ways And My thoughts than your thoughts.[12]

His thinking defies our thinking. As He is so far above us, we labor with difficulty to comprehend what He is doing and why. That conundrum should come as no surprise to us – He tells us to expect as much. He is wholly other, and His ways are informed by *all* of truth. Ours are at best only informed by a very small fraction of truth, and only that which He has chosen to reveal.

---

[10] Hebrews 12:5-7.
[11] Exodus 20:5.
[12] *New American Standard Bible: 1995 Update* (La Habra, CA: The Lockman Foundation, 1995), Is 55:8–9.

In light of His vast superiority, it is no wonder that Paul rebukes our attempts to hold God to account when he says, "who are you, O, man, who answers back to God? The thing molded will not say to the molder, 'Why did you make me like this?' will it?"[13] In understanding any challenging passage or situation this must be our starting point – a recognition that God's ways are higher than our own. As Solomon reminds us, wisdom and knowledge begin with the fear of the Lord[14] – the right perspective of Him and response to Him. In other words, for Solomon, the most foundational epistemological premise is that God holds the keys to knowledge and wisdom, and that we must go to Him to gain them, otherwise we are borrowing His truths blindly. In that blindness we may still arrive at great understanding, but we won't be able grasp the *meaning* or the broad context of such knowledge.

The atheist thinker, George Smith, suggests that, "The belief that god is basically unknowable is the most important epistemological element of theistic belief. It is shared by all theists to some extent, who disagree only with regard to what degree, if any, god's nature can be known.[15] Smith further argues that "When God's attributes are pushed to the limits of absurdity, the Christian invariably falls back on man's inability to comprehend God. If the atheist complains that omnipotence is impossible, or that a benevolent God cannot be reconciled with the existence of evil in the universe, the Christian retreats into the unknowable god of agnosticism. Man, we are told, cannot

---

[13] Romans 9:20.
[14] Proverbs 1:7, 9:10.
[15] George Smith, *Atheism: The Case Against God* (New York: Prometheus Books, 1989), 29.

understand the ways of God."¹⁶ For Smith, this represents the central irrationality of theism and has an important result:

> We have now uncovered an important principle: Scratch the surface of a Christian and you will find an agnostic. The Christian God is simply the agnostic god with window dressing. The characteristics of the Christian God are a first line of defense against agnosticism, but the Christian will eventually seek refuge in the claim that his God, like the agnostic god, is unknowable. If this is true—if the God of Christianity collapses into agnosticism under scrutiny—then the Christian is no better off than the agnostic, and our previous criticisms of agnosticism will apply to Christianity as well. The Christian will be expressing the inexpressible, thinking about the unthinkable, and presenting knowledge of the unknowable. If this is the case, we must ask the Christian to "retreat into silence" or relinquish his belief. And we shall also have demonstrated why Christian theism must be rejected by any person with even a shred of respect for reason.¹⁷

Smith concludes that if a Christian can't really know God to a degree that Smith approves, then the Christian is no more enlightened than an agnostic, so Smith demands the Christian should shut up (retreat into silence), or better – abandon his or her faith.

Smith is correct in one sense – that there is a limit to God's knowability. Isaiah 55 makes that clear enough. But Smith's diagnosis implies that the Bible is somewhat clumsy in its presentation of God. Somehow it is attempting to speak intelligently about God, but it falls short in revealing too little for people to have a reasonable knowledge of God that would warrant their faith. From Smith's perspective, the Bible

---

[16] Ibid., 31.
[17] Ibid., 34.

attempts a great and worthy God, but arrives at an incomprehensible jumble unworthy of anyone's faith.

What Smith fails to recognize is the *deliberate* limitations of special revelation. In Isaiah 55:8-9, God is the one speaking. He is the one who establishes the limits of what may or may not be understood about Him. Note Paul's assertion that God's invisible attributes, His eternal power, and His divine nature are *clearly seen*, being understood through what has been made.[18] That isn't referring to special revelation (the Bible), that is talking about general revelation – God's communication through His creation. So, God reveals a great deal about Himself in His creation, so much so, in fact, that all are without excuse.[19] That is sufficient knowledge for the purpose which God intends it.

Further, Solomon explains that eternity is set in the hearts of humanity, yet so as they will not discover all the works of God.[20] He has determined to make some significant aspects of Himself self-evident to people, but He has also held some things back. Jesus later says that the very meaning of life is to know God.[21] Paul prays in Ephesians 1:15-23 that believers will grow in the knowledge of Christ, to the extent that they will know His hope and His power. Solomon again encourages people to pursue wisdom so that they will discern the fear of the Lord and discover His knowledge.[22] Moreover, that knowledge comes from God's word.[23]

---

[18] Romans 1:20.
[19] Ibid.
[20] Ecclesiastes 3:11.
[21] John 17:3.
[22] Proverbs 2:5.
[23] 2:6.

In Paul's Letter to the Romans, he details the incredible works of God, as God had revealed them. Paul occasionally refers to the mysteries that are now revealed.[24] Yet, after explaining the intricacies of the mercies of God, he challenges believers to base their entire lives on what God has done – to present their bodies a living and holy sacrifice.[25] Does it sound like Paul has confidence that God is as knowable as God wants to be – and knowable enough for us to live according to that knowledge? At the same time, while Paul tells us to live based on what is revealed about God, he also remarks beautifully (just before that exhortation) how unsearchable and unfathomable are His ways.[26] Thanks be to God! If He didn't reveal Himself to us, we wouldn't know anything about Him, yet He did reveal quite a great deal.

Part of that knowledge helps us recognize that God is the potter, and His creation is the clay,[27] and just as the potter has the right of sovereignty over the clay, so God has that right over His creation. Isn't it odd then, that thinkers like Smith would suggest that the idea of God is irrational, and that He hasn't revealed enough of Himself for us to trust Him? As the Sovereign over His creation, He has the right to determine how much of Himself He will reveal, and how much He will keep to Himself. Further, we can recognize that in any case where there is a conflict in the ideas of God's sovereignty and our exercise of choice or volition, the solution is simple: God wins. As Paul says, nothing depends on the man who runs or the man who wills, but

---

[24] Romans 11:25, 16:25.
[25] 12:1-2.
[26] 11:33-36.
[27] 9:21.

on God who has mercy.[28] It seems fairly obvious from this passage that man does actually have will, or volition, but that volition does not trump God's sovereignty over creation. Amazingly, God is sovereign enough to use human volition as part of His plan – and He has revealed as much in passages like Romans 9. Thank God He has communicated these things to us and allowed us to know so much about Him – enough to know we are merely clay in the Potter's hands, and that the Potter has the right to hold us accountable as He wills, and as He communicates.

---

[28] 9:16.

54 The Sofa Rule

11
Hastening the Day, And Other Oddities

In Peter's second letter, he writes to remind believers of who they are in Christ, the future that is their inheritance, and how that should impact their daily walk. One remarkable feature of the letter is Peter's modulation between emphasizing God's sovereign control – encouraging readers that they can have confidence in Him and in His promises – and human responsibility – challenging His readers to action.

In 1:3-4, he exhorts that believers already have been given all that they need for excellence in life. He has already provided through His promises what they need to become sharers (or partakers) in His nature. They are *already escaping* the world's corruption. God has started a process in believers, putting them in the position of newness of life in Christ, and in 1:5-8 believers are to be increasing daily in the practical expressions of that new life, and so be fruitful in applying the knowledge of Christ. The one who is lacking in those expressions hasn't lost the positional purification (or justification), but rather Peter describes in 1:9 that such a person "has a forgetfulness" about that purification. In these verses Peter brings to view two concurrent realities: God is sovereign, and the position He provides believers stands, and believers are responsible, being given a part in how that position is expressed. Further, after Peter reminds his readers of their eternally secure position because of what God has done, in 1:10 he tells them to be diligent (*spoudasate*) while being certain (*bebaion*) about their calling. God has already provided the one, and they are to supply the other. Peter shows this same dualistic thinking in his own life – he has certainty of the imminence of his death, because of what God had revealed to him,[1] and is at the same time striving to be diligent while he has opportunity.[2]

In chapter three Peter introduces another topic in which both the sovereignty of God and human responsibility are in play. He recounts a commonly asked question of those who wonder why Jesus hasn't yet returned.[3] Things continue as they have, without any sign of changing. The longstanding status quo seems to imply God is not sovereign or even active at all. Peter responds by reminding readers that God created in the past, He judged in the past, and He will judge yet again in the future.[4] Peter explains that for God time is inconsequential,[5] and that His delay is not slowness but patience. He then makes the magnificent statement that He is "not wishing that any should perish but for all to come to repentance.[6] The issue here is not necessarily with the "who," as Peter makes clear that the

---

[1] 2 Peter 1:14.
[2] 1:15.
[3] 3:4.
[4] 3:5-7.
[5] 3:8.
[6] 3:9.

patience is toward "you." Every occurrence of the second person plural pronoun in Peter's letter is a clear reference to believers. The issue here is the "when." He is purposefully delaying His return. Still, because His return is certain, believers ought to conduct themselves in view of that, and in so doing Peter casually remarks that we are even "hastening the coming of the day of God."[7]

God is deliberately waiting with an end goal in mind, and the timing of His return is impacted *by what believers do*. Peter offers no explanation for how God can sovereignly be executing a plan toward its fulfillment and at the same time at least the timing of that fulfillment can be influenced by the actions of those who believe in Him. Peter doesn't even seem phased by the tension between God's sovereignty and human responsibility, or the certainty of God's plan and His design for humanity to add an element of uncertainty in timing – at least from our perspective. Peter doesn't seem to have any concern that his readers might be troubled by such a paradox. Perhaps the simple reason for his confidence is that the two concepts are not contradictory, and their coexistence is just basic reality. God is in control and He allows our actions to be influential in the unfolding of His plan. No big deal.

God isn't bound by time, nor is He bound by the false choice of either maintaining sovereignty or granting human volition and influence. As is the case in quite a few theological controversies, the answer is neither door number one nor door number two – when we open the third door, we discover human volition is simply an aspect or expression of His creative design

---

[7] 3:12.

and sovereignty over His creation. No big deal for a Sovereign Creator, simply another day at the office.

PART 2:

THEOLOGICAL, PHILOSOPHICAL, AND PRACTICAL IMPLICATIONS

60   The Sofa Rule

12
The Intersection of Philosophy, Theology, and Worldview

A worldview is the perspective through which one views the world. By definition, a Biblical worldview is derived exegetically from the pages of the Bible. Philosophy and theology have long been perceived as rivals in worldview, but if we define those terms lexically and through a Scriptural lens, then we find no friction between the two disciplines. In fact, the two are complementary.

Philosophy as a discipline is recognized as "the systematic and critical study of fundamental questions that arise both in everyday life and through the practice of other disciplines."[1] Philosophy *the discipline* is often confused with philosophy *as a worldview*. The discipline is informed by the worldview (or the perspective by which the philosopher is viewing philosophy), but the discipline is distinct from worldview. For example, many of the early Greek philosophers set out to find answers to life's great questions using *only* naturalistic evidences. To their credit, they were in part

---

[1] "What is Philosophy?" Brown University, viewed at https://www.brown.edu/academics/philosophy/undergraduate/philosophy-what-and-why.

motivated by a desire to move away from superstition and unwarranted belief in a pantheon that was hardly explanatory. The naturalistic worldview of these thinkers shaped much of what we understand as philosophical inquiry, but it is important to note that it was their worldview that was naturalistic, not the discipline of philosophy itself.

The Apostle Paul cautions against any philosophy that would deceive, and contrasts between philosophy rooted in humanism (or according to the traditions of men) and philosophy rooted in Christ.[2] Paul's warning illustrates the distinction between a worldview and the discipline. A Biblical philosophy is one that acknowledges Christ's identity,[3] explanatory value,[4] and authority as Creator.[5] One inference from Paul's statement is that one's philosophy is correct insofar as it is Christologically correct. For Paul, theology and philosophy are intertwined.

The Biblical worldview applied to philosophy helps us understand philosophy in its lexical sense as the love of wisdom, and points us to the first principles of that wisdom as the proper perspective of and response to God,[6] and to the source of that wisdom as the word of God.[7] As theology is *the study of God*, the theological discipline of Bibliology (the study of the Bible) is paramount at this introductory stage of worldview and philosophy.

The process of doing philosophy includes beginning with answering questions related to how we acquire knowledge, truth, and certainty. These are questions of epistemology. Every worldview (and philosophy) must first identify its source of authority – who or what it will trust to provide knowledge, truth, and certainty. In the Biblical worldview, that source is God revealed through Scripture. Another vital component of

---

[2] Colossians 2:8.
[3] 2:9.
[4] 2:10a.
[5] 2:10b.
[6] Proverbs 1:7, 9:10.
[7] 2:6.

epistemological enquiry is how that source of authority is interpreted or understood – *hermeneutics*. Without a proper hermeneutic framework as the capstone to epistemology, it is difficult to find either transparency or consistency in a worldview.

Once the epistemological questions are answered, there is a matrix for addressing the metaphysical questions – those questions pertaining to the nature of reality. Metaphysics considers four major areas: ontology (the nature of existence), axiology (the nature of value), teleology (the nature of design and purpose), and eschatology (the nature of the future). These four areas of study overlap the major categories of theology (Bibliology is not in this list, as it is addressed in Epistemology):

- Theology Proper – the study of God the Father
- Christology – the study of Christ
- Pneumatology – the study of the Spirit of God
- Angelology – the study of angels, demons, and the spiritual world
- Natural Theology – the study of nature as substance (natural sciences) and as revelatory device
- Anthropology – the study of humanity and everything directly related to human existence (for example, the discipline of psychology would fit in this category)
- Hamartialogy – the study of sin and its impact
- Soteriology – the study of salvation and its impact
- Ecclesiology – the study of the assembly we call the church
- Israelology – the study of the nation of Israel, as unique and chosen, and where it fits in God's plan
- Eschatology – the study of last things, the future, and ultimate fulfillment of Biblical promises

Each of these theological topics fit within the greater discipline of metaphysics, and without attention to each one, the overall metaphysical understanding would be woefully incomplete.

Epistemology and Metaphysics provides the *is* of philosophy – the descriptive aspects of reality. Flowing from that *is* there is an *ought*. Ethics provides the *ought* on an individual scale, and socio-political on a societal scale. In a Biblical worldview, there are two major categories of ethics – one for unbelievers (to become believers), and one for believers (to become more like Christ). Socio-political concepts round out the philosophical discussion, as various distinctives in society are considered, including the nations in general, Israel specifically, the universal church, and local fellowships of the universal church.

A reasonably ordered philosophy, seen from a Biblical perspective, overlaps major theological concepts and provides a broad and comprehensive backdrop for enquiry in any discipline. In a Biblical approach, philosophy and theology are interconnected, and in some cases even interchangeable. This close relationship between the two disciplines of philosophy and theology invites inquisitiveness and pursuit of knowledge in every area, and nothing about the Biblical approach to these disciplines would restrict or de-incentivize learning and discovery. Approaching any discipline from a Biblical worldview perspective invites the enquirer to examine thoroughly, and to "taste and see that the Lord is good."[8]

---

[8] Psalm 34:8.

13
The Beautiful Paradox:
God's Fathomability and Unknowability

In response to the question of whether or not science makes belief in God obsolete, Christopher Hitchens (who ultimately argues for the necessary obsolescence of God), suggested that, "It will not do to say, in reply to this, that the lord moves in mysterious ways. Those who dare to claim to be his understudies and votaries and interpreters must either accept the cruelty and the chaos or disown it: they cannot pick and choose between the warmly benign and the frigidly indifferent."[1]

Hitchens' essential argument against theism is that the theistic explanation was conceived in the infancy of humanity during its most ignorant stages and that as humanity has matured somewhat, there are better (or at least equally

---

[1] Christopher Hitchens, "No, but it should." in *Does science make belief in God obsolete? A Templeton Conversation* (West Conshohocken, PA: John Templeton Foundation), 15, viewed at https://andrewjmonaco.files.wordpress.com/2012/10/templeton-science-religion.pdf.

plausible) explanations than to appeal to the divine. One of the problems Hitchens and others identify with theism is that they cannot justify the existence of evil with the existence of a *good* divine sovereign. In the above remark, Hitchens argues that the believer cannot appeal to the unfathomability of God as a blanket explanation for the behavior of God, suggesting that even "morality shudders at the thought of god." In short, God allows (or causes) things that don't square with Hitchens' morality, and the oft' repeated explanation by believers is that *we simply can't know God's reasons*. The appeal to God's unfathomability is more or less an argument from silence. Thus, some conclude that if He exists at all, God is a jerk. However, the problem that Hitchens and others identify is addressed by Paul's doxological paradox in Romans 11:33-36.

In Romans 1-11 Paul explains in great detail the remarkable things God has done in order to save people. He introduces the "good news" in 1:16-17, describing it as His ability to save people of every ethnicity (notice the order of priority listed in 1:16) through faith or belief in Christ. Chapters 1-3:20 consider the universal need for God's grace, as there are none righteous, not even one.[2]

Beginning in 3:21 Paul explains that the righteousness of God has been revealed in Christ, as the Hebrew Scriptures had preannounced, and all who believe in Him are credited with His righteousness and are thus spared from the wages of sin. Romans 3:21-8:39 describes the implications of this salvation, noting that believers have peace with God,[3] that this was provided for even when we were enemies of God,[4] that because

---

[2] Romans 3:10.
[3] 5:1.
[4] 5:8.

we are alive to God we are dead to sin,[5] and thus we should no longer be governed by sin, that there is a conflict between the believer and his or her flesh,[6] and that because the believer's new position in Christ was accomplished by Christ there is no condemnation and there is an eternal security for the believer.[7]

Chapters 9-11 illustrate that God is faithful by recounting His purpose and future plans for the nation of Israel. God made promises during Old Testament times, and He will keep them. Consequently, the church-age believer can trust Him when He makes promises to them.

As Paul concludes that incredible panorama of "the mercies of God"[8] throughout the first eleven chapters of Romans, he interjects a magnificent doxology in 11:33-36:

> Oh, the depth of the riches both of the wisdom and knowledge of God! How unsearchable are His judgments and unfathomable His ways! For who has known the mind of the Lord, or who became His counselor? Or who has first given to Him that it might be paid back to him again? For from Him and through Him and to Him are all things. To Him *be* the glory forever. Amen.

After spending eleven chapters mining the depths of the applied wisdom of God, Paul recognizes that there is a limit to what can be understood about God. It is as if he is saying in this doxology that the aspects of God that are revealed in these eleven chapters are just the tip of the iceberg and that there is so much more to God than what is revealed here. Still, revelation is the key. Recall that God's righteousness has been revealed through faith (1:17), and these chapters of the Romans' letter focus on

---

[5] 6:1-7.
[6] 7:14-25.
[7] 8:1, 28-30.
[8] 12:1.

what that faith means. These aspects of the revealed righteousness of God are incredible and elegant, and grounds for praising God. Paul's response here is fitting.

Another important aspect of the doxology is the appeal in 11:34-35 to God's sovereign rights as the Creator. As He owes no one anything, and is the sovereign Creator, He has the authority to write the rules and to apply His wisdom as He sees fit. Some of that He has chosen to reveal, some He hasn't. Paul's doxology provides a backdrop for the important truth that what God has revealed is knowable, but there is much He has not revealed. God is unfathomable to His creation,[9] yet knowable insofar as He has revealed Himself.[10] This is the beautiful paradox.

To assume that we can know enough of God to morally critique Him assumes also that we also have some base of moral authority from which to judge Him. Paul leaves no room for this when he reproves those who would judge God. He walks the critic down a Socratic path in 9:14-20: "What shall we say then? There is no injustice with God, is there? May it never be!…You will say to me then, "Why does He still find fault? For who resists His will?"… On the contrary, who are you, O man, who answers back to God? The thing molded will not say to the molder, "Why did you make me like this," will it?"

It is somewhat ironic that God actually uses human understanding of the science of the physical world as an example of His own superiority over humanity. For example, He asks Job, "Can you send forth lightnings that they may go and say to you, 'Here we are'?"[11] Science has not made God obsolete until it provides humanity complete and total control of nature –

---

[9] Isaiah 55:8-9.
[10] Proverbs 2:6, Ecclesiastes 3:11.
[11] Job 38:35.

including creating *ex nehilo* and having the ability to conquer death. When these conditions are met, then perhaps humanity will be in a position to stand as a peer to God, but until then, "who are you O man, who answers back to God?"

The beautiful paradox has significant implications. God is knowable insofar as He has revealed Himself, and He has the sovereignty to determine what to reveal and what not to reveal. Further, insofar as He has not revealed Himself, He is unfathomable, and infinitely beyond us. This is what makes the paradox beautiful: the transcendent Master of the universe has reached out to His creation and is intimately involved in it. He revealed Himself in nature, in Scripture, and ultimately, in His Son.

It is no mere coincidence that Jesus Christ came demonstrating His power over nature to show that He had sovereign rights over His creation, so that when He said, "the believing one has eternal life,"[12] we could have confidence not only in His word on its own merit (which would be enough), but also in the science that testifies of His authority to make such claims.

---

[12] John 6:37.

The Sofa Rule

14

I Was Born That Way:
A Biblical Teleological Argument For Identity, Sex, and Sexuality[1]

Matthew Vines and others supporting the LGBTQ perspective have argued for a *Moral Permissive View* on sexual orientation. The argument has been two-tiered: (1) that the more traditional *Moral Prohibitive View* is based on six Scriptures that are ultimately not relevant to the present discussion, and (2) that in the absence of Biblical data for or against healthy homosexual relationships, Christians should choose the more inclusive, affirming approach rather than condemn such relationships.

In order to advance the discussion beyond the stalemate of these two models, and in order to apply a solidly Biblical hermeneutic, this paper proposes a third approach: *The Inherent Design Model.* This third model considers God's particular design for identity, sex, and sexuality in Genesis 1 and 2, Jesus' affirmation of that model in Matthew 19, Paul's

---

[1] Initially presented to the Bible Faculty Summit, International Baptist College and Seminary, Chandler, Arizona, August 7, 2019.

recognition in 1 Corinthians 7 that the design offers only one inherent alternative (celibacy), and his explanation in Romans 1 of other alternatives as violating God's design. The *Inherent Design Model* concludes that LGBTQ applications violate God's design, and the model contextualizes the ethical implications so that believers can respond in a way that honors all people (including LGBTQ) and can demonstrate the love of Christ while not compromising Biblical truth.

INTRODUCTION

In a 2014 episode of the TV series Blue Bloods, a dialogue between a reporter and the series' Catholic lead character, NYPD Commissioner, Frank Reagan drew attention to the perception of the RCC's stance on same-sex relationships:

> *Reporter: The Catholic Church condemns homosexuality as a sin and the Commissioner is famously Catholic. How do you line up your anti-gay faith with your role as an equal-opportunity employer?*
> *Reagan: What my men and women do in private is their own business.*
> *Reporter: So you only condemn homosexuality on a Sunday?*
> *Reagan: Well, I do believe that the Church is a little behind the times on this, but then I still miss the Latin Mass.*[2]

While numerous commentators disagreed with the show's representation of the RCC view of homosexuality,[3] the dialogue

---

[2] Blue Bloods, "Burning Bridges ," Directed by John Behring, Written by Willie Reale, CBS, October 10, 2014.
[3] E.g., Jane Chastain, "Blue Bloods Has People of Faith Seeing Red," JaneChastain.com, October 15, 2014, viewed at https://janechastain.com/2014/10/15/blood-bloods-has-people-of-faith-seeing-red/, and Susan E. Wills, "Blue Bloods" Blooper Exposes Confusion about the Church and Gays," Aletia.org, October 12, 2014,

illustrated the friction present even among the most ardent followers regarding issues related to same-sex relationships. What once was a din has now become a crescendo of public opinion that the Judeo-Christian model for sexuality is no longer correct or beneficial.

The Barna Group reports that "the decades-old trend that Christianity is irrelevant is giving way to the notion that Christianity is bad for society."[4] More than 80% of adults in the US believe it is very or somewhat extreme to refuse to serve someone because the customer's lifestyle conflicts with their beliefs. Between 50 and 79% believe it is very or somewhat extreme to believe that sexual relationships between people of the same sex are morally wrong. The same percentage perceives it to be equally extreme to teach children that sexual relationships between people of the same sex are morally wrong.[5] The increasing divide between culture and Christianity is perhaps more evident in the area of same-sex relationships than in any other context. Just as same-sex advocates have been active in trying to expose the disconnect, the Christian community has engaged the issue, but has neither been definitive nor particularly effective in holding back the groundswell. In 2003, for example, 12% of Protestants considered same-sex relationships to be morally acceptable, up to 15% in 2013. Among Catholics the 2003 number was 19%, and nearly doubled to 37% in 2013. In both groups a growing

---

viewed at https://aleteia.org/2014/10/12/blue-bloods-blooper-exposes-confusion-about-the-church-and-gays/.

[4] The Barna Group, "Five Ways Christianity is Increasingly Viewed as Extremist," Barna.com, February 23, 2015, viewed at https://www.barna.com/research/five-ways-christianity-is-increasingly-viewed-as-extremist/.

[5] Ibid.

minority approves of same-sex relationships, while those who associate with no faith approve homosexuality at a rate of 71%.[6] As faith is perceived to be increasingly irrelevant, it is fairly clear that the trend toward acceptance of same-sex relationships will continue.

Among Evangelicals there are two prominent arguments, one for and one against the morality and acceptability of same-sex relationships. The Moral Permissive View, proposed by advocates of homosexuality and supported by a cultural distance argument, postulates that because there are no explicit prohibitions in the New Testament, the overwhelmingly negative mood toward homosexuality is cultural, and is specifically targeting inappropriate homosexual activity, and is not addressing committed and monogamous homosexual. On the other hand, in more traditional Evangelical circles, the longstanding Moral Prohibitive perspective abides, supported by legal restrictions in the Mosaic Law that are presupposed and uncontradicted in the New Testament and thus remain applicable for today.

This writer suggests that a third approach, an Inherent Design View, provides a superior argument, in that it (1) is more methodologically consistent with a literal grammatical-historical approach to the Scriptures, (2) draws exegetically justifiable conclusions about the character of God and the origin of morality, and (3) recognizes the progress of revelation allowing for both a cogency and discontinuity in God's revelation on the matter. If the Inherent Design approach accurately

---

[6] The Barna Group, "America's Change of Mind on Same-Sex Marriage and LGBTQ Rights," Barna.com, July 3, 2013, viewed at https://www.barna.com/research/americas-change-of-mind-on-same-sex-marriage-and-lgbtq-rights/.

represents the Biblical record, then readers can have confidence even if the Biblical record itself is contrary to current streams of prevailing culture. In that case, the solution would not be found in conforming the Bible to culture (as does the Moral Permissive View), nor in condemning culture based on Mosaic norms (as does the Moral Prohibitive View), but rather in recognizing the Creator as the Sovereign and Designer, to Whom we should look for our identity, definition, and purpose.

In any consideration of such matters of great controversy, it is appropriate to remember why we are engaging the discussion in the first place. Paul provides an important preface to such discussions when he reminds Timothy that "the goal of our instruction is love from a pure heart and a good conscience and a sincere faith."[7] The discussion, rightly engaged, ought to produce an expression of Christlike love that is rooted in purity, goodness, and sincerity. In other words, love is the vital conclusion – not love in a general sense, but rather a certain kind of love – a prescribed kind of love designed by our Creator for accomplishing His purposes. As we compare the merits and limitations of these three perspectives, we are reminded that there is no room for hatred of or disrespect toward people,[8] nor is there room for compromising truth,[9] lest we show hatred of and disrespect toward our Creator.

---

[7] 1 Timothy 1:5. Unless otherwise indicated, all Scripture references are from the NASB, copyright by the Lockman Foundation.
[8] 1 Peter 2:17.
[9] Ephesians 4:15.

MORAL PERMISSIVE VIEW
(CULTURAL DISTANCE THEOLOGY)

Built on the essential yet unstated premise that God cannot or will not hold a person morally accountable for what they do not choose, Matthew Vines asserts that "Gay people have a natural, permanent orientation toward those of the same sex. It is not something they choose, and it's not something they can change. They aren't abandoning or rejecting heterosexuality – that's never an option for them to begin with."[10] Vines adds an emotional appeal, emphasizing the hurt caused by viewing homosexuality as wrong:

> Being different is no crime. Being gay is not a sin. And for a gay person to desire and pursue love and marriage and family is no more selfish or sinful than when a straight person desires and pursues the very same things. The Song of Songs tells us that King Solomon's wedding day was "the day his heart rejoiced." To deny to a small minority of people, not just a wedding day, but a lifetime of love and commitment and family is to inflict on them a devastating level of hurt and anguish.[11]

Elsewhere, Vines characterizes Paul's negativity toward homosexual activity as targeting only a particular kind of behavior. Vines suggests that, "Paul is explicit that the same-sex behavior in this passage is motivated by lust. His description is similar to the common ancient idea that people "exchange" opposite-sex for same-sex relations because they are driven by

---

[10] Matthew Vines, "The Gay Debate: The Bible and Homosexuality," March 10, 2012, viewed at https://www.youtube.com/watch?v=ezQjNJUSraY.
[11] Ibid.

out-of-control desire, not because they have a different sexual orientation."[12]

Vines' advocacy of permissiveness is rooted in three key factors. First, Vines appeals to cultural distance – the idea that the culture that the Bible is addressing in its negative connotations of homosexuality is not the responsible culture of same-sex love that Vines seeks to exonerate. Second, God has an obligation to respect human free will, and can not (or will not) judge humanity for that which is not chosen. Finally, Vines' strongest and perhaps most effective appeal is to the heartache that he purports is brought on by condemnations of same-sex relationships. *Note that the desired outcome for Vines is not merely tolerance, but rather acceptance. Anything less will not resolve a devastating level of hurt and anguish.* Vines' argument is rhetorically powerful. Who would want to cause hurt and anguish? Certainly, no one who holds to any kind of Christian ethic. However, claims of injury of this sort are difficult if not impossible to prove, and they don't make for strong arguments, outside of their emotional appeal. Vines' other two premises, on the other hand, are perhaps more grounded in historic philosophical argument.

The idea that homosexuality is not a choice and thus cannot be condemned on moral grounds cuts to the heart of whether or not humanity is a completely free moral agent. While there has not, as of yet been provided any scientific data to suggest that homosexuality is actually individually predetermined, determinism is important to Vines' argument.

---

[12] Matthew Vines, "Debating Bible Verses on Homosexuality," New York Times, June 8, 2015, viewed at https://www.nytimes.com/interactive/2015/06/05/us/samesex-scriptures.html.

The premise holds that if God were to judge that which is not chosen, then His justice could be questioned. But the flaw in this assumption is especially apparent in Romans 5. In that context, Paul acknowledges that Adam's sin resulted in the sinfulness of all humanity.[13] Thus, people who did not choose to be born were brought into this life, born into death and separation from God. They did not individually *first* choose against God, they were already by nature children of wrath,[14] enemies of God,[15] and helpless.[16] God holds humanity morally accountable for what they don't choose. Consequently, even if the claim that homosexuality is inherited and not chosen was demonstrated to be true, that would not invalidate God's sovereign right to hold His creation accountable on His own terms.

Vines' cultural distance premise is well voiced by Justin Cannon, who suggests that the Bible isn't addressing a culture of honorable and respectful homosexuality, but rather an abusive form of same-sex activity:

> ...the Bible really does not fully address the topic of homosexuality. Jesus never talked about it. The prophets never talked about it. In Sodom homosexual activity is mentioned within the context of rape (raping angels nonetheless), and in Romans 1:24-27 we find it mentioned within the context of idolatry (Baal worship) involving lust and dishonorable passions. 1 Corinthians 6:9 and 1 Timothy 1:10 talk about homosexual activity in the context of prostitution and possibly pederasty. Nowhere does the

---

[13] Romans 5:12-19 states six times explicitly that Adam's sin caused all to be in sin.
[14] Ephesians 2:3.
[15] Romans 5:8-10.
[16] Romans 5:6.

Bible talk about a loving and committed homosexual relationship.[17]

In one sense, Cannon is right – there is minimal Biblical discussion of homosexuality compared to other issues. There are six clear references to same-sex activity in Scripture,[18] and yet there are forty-four mentions of adultery, thirty-five references to lust, seventy-two instances of deceit, and thirty-eight instances of jealousy. If the Scripture has so little to say on the matter, why the controversy? Cannon suggests that the six same-sex references are generally mishandled (by those advocating the Moral Prohibitive View), even with respect to the terminology used.

Raymond Hays helps interlocutors understand the significance of the terms chosen, arguing that the verbiage is clear enough to invalidate the cultural distance premise. Hays' comments in that regard are worth noting here:

> The word *malakoi* is not a technical term meaning "homosexuals" (no such term existed in either Greek or Hebrew), but it appears as pejorative slang to describe the "passive" partners – often young boys – in homosexual activity. The other word, *arsenokoitai*, is not found in any extant Greek text earlier than 1 Corinthians. Some scholars have suggested that its meaning is uncertain, but Robin Scroggs has shown that the word is a translation of the Hebrew *mishkav zakur* ("lying with a male"), derived directly from Leviticus 18:22 and 20:13 and used in rabbinic texts to refer to homosexual intercourse. The Septuagint (Greek Old Testament) of Leviticus 20:13 reads, "Whoever lies with a man as with a woman [*meta arsenos koiten gynaikos*], they have done an

---

[17] Justin Cannon, "The Bible, Christianity and Homosexuality," GayChurch.org, viewed at https://www.gaychurch.org/homosexuality-and-the-bible/the-bible-christianity-and-homosexuality/.
[18] Genesis 19, Leviticus 18:22, 20:13, Romans 1, 1 Corinthians 6:9, and 1 Timothy 1:10.

abomination" (my translation). This is almost certainly the idiom from the noun *arsenokoitai* was coined. Thus, Paul's use of the term presupposes and reaffirms the holiness code's condemnation of homosexual acts.[19]

If Hays is right, then the terms employed in the New Testament passages are enough to include all homosexual activity, and not just the kinds that Vines and Cannon would perceive as abusive.

Still, perhaps the strongest assertion for the Moral Permissive View is simply that no explicit rule prohibiting same-sex activity is ever given in the New Testament. However, to state the positive assertion of Biblical permissiveness on those grounds would be to postulate an argument from silence. This would be the same (il)logical maneuver employed in perceiving Christian ethics as permissive of murder because there is not one direct prohibition of murder in the New Testament. The nearest to any such direct prohibition are the several references to Mosaic Law from Jesus and James, and it is worth noting that neither actually stated the mandate on its own merit outside of the Mosaic context. If homosexuality can be absolved this way, then so can murder.

While the aforementioned grounds for the Moral Permissive argument are persuasive to some, their limitations are not difficult to identify. Nonetheless, the emotional appeal and the simple peer pressure that results is perhaps the most persuasive of all. It is ironic, in the view of this writer, that kindness, compassion, and respect remain the most valuable influencers in favor of same-sex activity. Still, it is important to note that if these virtues are misplaced in advocating for homosexuality, then their persuasiveness is a mirage and even

---

[19] Richard Hays, *The Moral Vision of the New Testament:* (San Francisco, CA: HarperOne, 1996), 382.

a deception. Kindness, compassion, and respect must be rooted in truth – just as the kind of love that drives orthopraxy is a particular kind of love – from a pure heart and a good conscience and a sincere faith.

MORAL PROHIBITIVE VIEW (LEGALITY THEOLOGY)

For the Roman Catholic thinker, the Moral Prohibitive View is a good fit. Historical tradition is clear about the moral illegality of homosexual activity: "Basing itself on Sacred Scripture, which presents acts of homosexuality as acts of grave depravity, tradition has always declared that 'homosexual acts are intrinsically disordered.' They are contrary to the natural law..."[20] Commendably, the *Catechism* calls those who might consider themselves homosexuals to chastity.[21] As the appeal to historical theology implies, there is a longstanding prohibition, about which, there has been little debate until more recently, as the RCC seeks to maintain cultural relevance. For the Reformed/Covenant thinker, the Moral Prohibitive View is the most natural fit, consistent with the theological hermeneutic that governs Reformed/Covenant understanding of the applicability of the Mosaic Law for the church today. In this view, because God legislates from His character, His legislation cannot change (as His character is immutable). Consequently, the Law *must* remain in effect.

Whereas advocates of the Moral Permissive View read the Bible through the lens of culture, proponents of the Moral Prohibitive View focus on several passages of Scripture through the lens of theology and tradition (or at least certain

---

[20] *Catholic Catechism*, Part 3, Section 2, Chapter 2, Article 6, 2357.
[21] Ibid., 2359.

philosophical pre-commitments). While some of the several references are not definitive, it is the Mosaic legal references that are usually given the most weight in this approach.

Setting the context, and perhaps providing precedent, Genesis 19 records the judgment of Sodom, and while 19:5 records an attempted homosexual gang rape, homosexuality is not identified in the context as the reason for the impending judgment. In fact, it is obvious that the judgment was already on its way before the citizens of Sodom sought to commit that particular offense. Further, God Himself attributes the guilt of Sodom as "arrogance, abundant food and careless ease, but she did not help the poor and needy."[22] While He adds that also "they committed abominations,"[23] He does not specify the nature of those abominations. Jude 7 gets closer to directly addressing Sodom's homosexuality, citing "gross immorality" and going after strange flesh (*sarkos heteras*), but arguably the latter reference could be speaking of the angelic nature of the would-be victims. Still, Genesis 19 seems to set a clear precedent for the negativity of homosexual activity, but the passage is not definitive for that purpose.

Leviticus 18:22 and 20:13 contain the only clear Biblical prohibitions of or direct mandates against same-sex sexual activity. This context is part of the Law of Moses, and the Mosaic Covenant which was made with "the house of Jacob and the sons of Israel."[24] The question is whether or not mandates found within a conditional, targeted covenant are broadly applicable and ethically binding today. Advocates of the Moral Prohibitive View are generally clear that these mandates are binding. The

---

[22] Ezekiel 16:49.
[23] 16:50.
[24] Exodus 19:3.

essential premise here is that because the Law emanates from the character of God, the Law can't change, and is thus still in effect. This premise reads these legal passages through the lens of the theological conclusion regarding the nature of authority and God's immutability.

Greg Bahnsen, for example, speaks of the "abiding validity of the Law,"[25] suggesting the threefold division of the Law (moral, ceremonial, civil), and arguing that all three parts are equally binding, as evidenced by Matthew 5:17. Bahnsen holds to a strong Reformed/Covenant perspective that *authority is law*. God legislates from His character and can do no other. Because God's character is immutable, so must His law be also. Consequently, Christians today are under the Law, otherwise, God has violated His own character. Bahnsen's strong version of continuity[26] has been referred to as *theonomy*. He explains the applicability of the Law in a way consistent with his methodology: "The accomplishment of redemption changes the way in which we observe the ceremonial law, and the change of culture and times alters the specific ways in which we observe the case laws. The cases are different but the same moral principles remain."[27]

David Jones himself outlines and elucidates a semi-continuity[28] understanding that he recognizes as the prevailing

---

[25] Greg Bahnsen, *Theonomy in Christian Ethics,* (Nacogdoches, TX: Covenant Media Press, 2002), ch. 2.
[26] My term to indicate that the Law continues to be in effect and broadly applicable.
[27] Greg Bahnsen, "The Faculty Discussion on Theonomy," Question 9, Reformed Theological Seminary, 1978, viewed at http://www.cmfnow.com/articles/pe192.htm.
[28] My term, to indicate that some of the Law continues and is applicable for today.

sentiment of the church.[29] Because Acts 15 ruled the ceremonial law not applicable to New Testament believer, and because the New Testament voices approval of non-theocratic governments, thus rendering the civil law non applicable,[30] the believer is only under the moral law for sanctification.[31] Jones' version, like Bahnsen's is rooted in the idea that authority is law, but Jones' is a weaker or gentler version that allows for two of the three divisions of the Mosaic Law to have been fulfilled, with the immutability of God reflected in the unchanging moral law of the Ten Commandments: "Since the Decalogue is a reflection of God's moral character, the norms codified in the Ten Commandments are universally applicable and demonstrable both before and after their issuance on Mount Sinai."[32]

The implications of this commonly held Reformed/Covenant perspective of the Law are illustrated well by Samuel Bolton, who suggests that "The law sends us to the gospel that we may be justified, and the gospel sends us to the law again to enquire what is our duty in being justified."[33] Bolton's comments underscore the importance of the Law as the believer's moral duty. As the Gospel is applied, its impact is universal, as Jones notes, "As the kingdom of God grows, then the gospel gradually counteracts and corrects the effects of sin in the world through the process of restoration and reconciliation...the gospel is no less comprehensive than the

---

[29] David Jones, *Introduction to Biblical Ethics* (Nashville: TN, B&H Academic, 2013), 76.
[30] E.g., Romans 13:1-5, 1 Peter 2:13-17.
[31] Jones, 139.
[32] Ibid.
[33] Samuel Bolton, *True Bonds of Christian Freedom* (London:UK, Banner of Truth, 1964), 80.

fall..."³⁴ So both Bolton and Jones (along with the majority of Reformed/Covenant thinkers) recognize the broad societal responsibility and impact of the Gospel applied in sanctification, that is through obedience to the Decalogue. Yet, there are two significant flaws with this approach.

First, how can the threefold division of the Law be justified? That division is not a textual one, but rather a theological device. How can it be said that the other two alleged aspects of the Law (ceremonial and civil) do not have moral components and are not equally as binding? In fact, this inconsistency is evident when advocates of this understanding appeal to Leviticus 18 and 20 as a lasting basis for rejection of same-sex activity. If that section is part of the civil law, or even the ceremonial, then upon what basis can it be justified that these principles remain? This creates a dilemma for the "authority is law" argument. If God legislates from His character, then how can He cleanse what He once declared unclean? If He does so, then His legislation can change. If He does not, then stay away from pork, shellfish, and mixing cloths carelessly!³⁵ Hays observes the problem:

> The Old Testament...makes no distinction between ritual law and moral law. The same section of the holiness code also contains, for instance, the prohibition of incest (Lev. 18:6-18). Is that a purity law or a moral law? Leviticus makes no distinction in principle. In each case, the church is tasked with discerning whether Israel's traditional norms remain in force for the new community of Jesus' followers. In order to see what decisions the early church made about this matter, we must turn to the New Testament.³⁶

---

³⁴ Jones, 64.
³⁵ E.g., Leviticus 11; Deuteronomy 22:11.
³⁶ Richard Hays, *The Moral Vision of the New Testament:* (San Francisco, CA: HarperOne, 1996), 382.

This begs the question that highlights the second significant flaw of the semi-continuity approach: Since James 2:10 tells us that if we stumble in one point we have violated all the Law, then how can any of these laws be changed without His express written or verbal direction? For example, notice how Jones handles the Sabbath, recognizing the tension between what was originally prescribed and what is the present habit of the church:

> For Christians, then, the Sabbath is a sign of redemption and, as such, it depicts the eternal rest they have received from Jesus in salvation...Keeping the Sabbath ought not to be a legalistic burden, characterized by lists of permitted and forbidden activities. Rather the Sabbath ought to be a joyous celebration and a blessing...In a specific sense the fourth commandment calls believers to observe a regular day of worship...not to observe the Sabbath, in either a broad or a specific sense, is to behave in a distinctly un-Christlike manner...in the NT...the early church moved the day of Sabbath observance to the first day of the week.[37]

The problems created by this statement are several. First, Jones characterizes without exegetical warrant the Sabbath as a sign of redemption for Christians, when it is expressly a sign between God and Israel.[38] Who determines the meaning of the sign if there is no textual data?[39] Second, he suggests the sabbath

---

[37] Jones, 166.
[38] Exodus 20:12.
[39] Hebrews 4 makes use of the Sabbath to illustrate a future reality for believers, but it does not at all invalidate the literal nature of the Sabbath, nor the carefully described sign component of the Sabbath for Israel (Ex 20:12, etc.), nor of the ethical requirement of the Sabbath within the Mosaic Law. Further, if the Law (even simply the moral aspect) is applicable for believers today, then the literal aspect must be

shouldn't be a legalistic burden, but the fourth commandment *was* a legal burden; he argues that it shouldn't be characterized by lists of permitted and forbidden activities, but in fact, that is exactly what the Sabbath was – and there are actually lists of forbidden activities.[40] Third, he suggests that the commandment is a call to observe a regular day of worship, when the text demands that it be a day of rest. Finally, he suggests that the church moved the day of Sabbath observance. Based on what authority could the church have done that, and where in Scripture do we see that actually happen? The semi-continuity view of the Law is problematic in light of James 2:10, and without some direct prescription, if the church moved the Sabbath then the church is guilty in the James 2:10 sense.

Now, if the Law was given to Israel only, has not been divided, but has been fulfilled in whole, then the two Leviticus passages cannot be seen as presently applicable prohibitions against homosexuality. If on the other hand, the Law has been given more broadly than simply to Israel, and has been divided, and has not been completely fulfilled, then ironically Christ ultimately has little if anything to do with Christian ethics, as His church is simply bound by Mosaic Law. And in the authority is law model, Christ couldn't change or fulfill the Law if He wanted to, lest He find Himself at odds with the character of His Father.

Besides the sticky conundrum of the applicability of the Law, there is another problem for the Moral Prohibitive View – outside of the Leviticus passages, there are simply no direct prohibitions of homosexual activity. Kevin DeYoung,

---

upheld, regardless of any metaphorical application of the Sabbath concept.
[40] Exodus 20:10, 35:2-3.

recognizing the challenges such an absence creates, crafts his argument on a cumulative case:

> There is nothing in the biblical text to suggest Paul or Moses or anyone else meant to limit the Scriptural condemnation of homosexual behavior. Likewise, there is no good reason to think from the thousands of homosexuality-related texts found in the Greco-Roman period that the blanket rejection of homosexual behavior found in the Bible can be redeemed by postulating an impassable cultural distance between our world and the ancient world. There is simply no positive case for homosexual practice in the Bible and no historical background that will allow us to set aside what has been the plain reading of Scripture for twenty centuries.[41]

While what DeYoung says here is not incorrect, it is – like the strongest argument for the Moral Permissive approach – an argument from silence. Essentially, DeYoung asserts that since the tone of Scripture is negative toward homosexuality, there is no positive case to be made favoring homosexuality. So far so good. But the implied conclusion is that there is a present day, practical prohibition in place. This argument from silence is better than that of the Moral Permissive View, because Moral Permissive has the arduous task of shedding the weight of Scripture's negativity toward homosexuality, while at least the Moral Prohibitive View lands on the correct side of the data. Still, DeYoung's argument is limited in that it does not provide certainty regarding what is the authentic Christian ethic for today. While both views suffer from the argument from silence

---

[41] Kevin DeYoung, "Not That Kind of Homosexuality," The Gospel Coalition, November 13, 2014, viewed at https://www.thegospelcoalition.org/blogs/kevin-deyoung/not-that-kind-of-homosexuality/.

as their *coup de gras*, the third view does not share that particular limitation.

INHERENT DESIGN VIEW
(DESIGN THEOLOGY)

When we read culture through the lens of the Bible, rather than the Bible through the lens of culture, we often find clarity. Genesis 19 (when coupled with Jude 7) and Leviticus 18:22 and 20:13 are all strongly negative toward same-sex activity. With forcefulness the Mosaic Law prohibits homosexual activity, however, in a literal grammatical-historical handling of Scriptures pertaining to the Mosaic Law, we must conclude that this was a conditional covenant exclusively for Israel, and that it was completely fulfilled in Christ, and now it serves the purpose as a tutor leading people to Christ.[42] The Christian is not under the Mosaic Law in any way – not for justification, and not for sanctification. Further, the Mosaic Law is not ethically applicable to the church beyond the purpose spelled out expressly in Scripture.

Consequently, it is evident that God *can* change (or fulfill) His legislation, and His use of that ability creates no friction for the literal grammatical-historical understanding, as God is clearly presented as Sovereign over all His creation. Thus, His authority is over law – law does not emanate from His character, it emanates from Him, when He chooses to give it. In this understanding there is no theological need for the threefold division of the Law, and since there is no exegetical warrant for inferring such a division, this approach is not guilty of eisegesis in this regard. Further, there is only one ethical standard for the

---

[42] Galatians 3:24-25.

Christian, and it is not the Mosaic Law (though it is referenced in that Law[43]), it is the holiness of God.[44] In light of God's holiness there are two distinct sets of ethical applications – one set for unbelievers (respect the sanctity of life[45] and believe in Christ[46]), and one set for believers (essentially, be holy). Unbelievers are not called to live holy lives according God's design – they are called to believe in their Creator, and then to walk in holiness. This concept helps us understand how 1 Corinthians 6:9 and 1 Timothy 1:10 are vitally connected to the design issue.

In 1 Corinthians 6:9 and 1 Timothy 1:10 are found characterizations that *arsenokoitai* are unrighteous and contrary to sound teaching, and as such, will not inherit the kingdom of God. The solution is also identified in 1 Corinthians 6:10 – be washed, sanctified, justified. Neither passage is teaching that homosexuality (or any other sin) is unforgiveable, on the contrary, some of the Corinthian believers were involved in exactly that, and yet they were redeemed. The implication is *not* that if one engages in any of these acts they will lose access to the Kingdom, rather the characterization is of the unrighteous (by nature) who express their unrighteousness in these particular symptomatic ways. The challenge in both of these passages is for believers not to live in the contrary absurdity as if they are positionally and by nature unrighteous, doing the deeds of unrighteousness – why should one who is redeemed and empowered by the Holy Spirit live like someone who will not inherit the Kingdom? That would be as illogical as

---

[43] E.g., Leviticus 11:45, 19:2, 20:7, 20:26, etc.
[44] 1 Peter 1:15.
[45] Genesis 9.
[46] Genesis 15:6, Habakkuk 2:4, John 20:30-31.

not presenting our bodies a living and holy sacrifice – because *that* is our logical service of worship.

Both of these passages are clear enough in describing homosexuality (along with lists of other activities) as displeasing to God. And if all we had were Genesis 19, Leviticus 18:22, 20:13, 1 Corinthians 6:9, and 1 Timothy 1:10, those passages alone would provide an incredible weight of clarity regarding the wrongness of homosexual activity. But when we examine the teleological component that God reveals in Scripture, especially in light of the culminating pericope of Romans 1, we can draw no other conclusion than homosexuality is a violation of God's created order,[47] and *that is why it is presented so negatively in the other passages.*

Six Teleological Elements

As we consider God's design for humanity, six aspects are evident. First is the *Design Question* – In Genesis 1:27 we read that God created man in His own image, in the image of God He created him; male (*zaqar*) and female (*negebah*) He created them. *But why did He create two sexes, male and female?* He could have done anything He wished, and yet it was His plan to create male and female. The simple answer is that there is no answer given in Scripture, so we leave it to the Designer to maintain His trade secrets. He has the authority to have chosen the design He did.

Second, we consider the *Design Deficiency*. God built into His creation an inherent deficiency. The first time in history we see anything referred to as not good, it is God's observation of Adam's aloneness. Adam did not have a helper (an opposite)

---

[47] Going far beyond Aquinas' and the RCC's appeal to natural law.

corresponding to him.[48] It is worth noting that the male sex already existed. Why didn't God just create another one of the same kind so that Adam would have companionship? Part of the answer may be seen in God's parading the animals before Adam so Adam could recognize how they were designed – male and female as counterpart, for procreation and other apparent reasons. Surely Adam would have also noticed the physical differences in the way the two sexes were built beyond their sexual capacities. Their anatomies were *designed* differently. The two would fulfill different roles and purposes, far beyond simply procreation. By contrast, Adam was at that point unique in that he had no counterpart.

Third, we see the *Design Resolution* in Genesis 2:18b-24. God said "I will make him a helper suitable for him."[49] That helper (*ezer*) was a woman. She was corresponding to or opposite (*neged*) him. Notice the prescriptive element in 2:24 – "For this reason a man shall leave his father and his mother and be joined to his wife; and they shall become one flesh." The proper expression of the design for togetherness is accomplished in marriage. It is stated simply and rooted in the created order.

Fourth, we encounter the *Design Affirmation*, as Jesus affirms the veracity and foundational nature of the creation story and how God Himself has joined man and woman.[50] Jesus affirmed the design in the created order, and affirmed monogamous, heterosexual marriage based on that design. If that is the design, then what of those who are not married? Are they in violation of that design? Are they dysfunctional in some way?

---

[48] Genesis 2:18.
[49] 2:18b.
[50] Matthew 19:4-6.

Paul addresses that question in the fifth point, providing the *Design Alternative*. In 1 Corinthians 7:8 and 17 Paul extols the high value of celibacy. Humanity is designed for marriage, but some are gifted, even called for celibacy. There are few giftings and callings actually spelled out in Scripture. It is rather remarkable that being single is referenced by both terms. The *designed* alternative for the *design* of marriage is to remain single or celibate – these are the two provided and positively stated paths for proper expression of sexuality.

One might ask at this point whether or not God has called or gifted any to homosexuality. If the design includes one positively stated alternative, then is it possible there is a second alternative? This is where the Inherent Design View avoids the argument from silence and instead argues from revelation that the single and exclusive alternative to the original design is revealed quantifiably in 1 Corinthians 7. Is it possible there is a second alternative? No, because the alternative is based on God's gifting and calling, and *to be certain* of God's gifting and calling in this context requires that He has revealed that there is such a gifting and calling. How can one walk in a supposed calling or gifting if they have no evidence that calling or gifting has come from Him? On what basis could they claim it is a calling or gifting at all? On the other hand, if one is married, they have that gifting and calling. If one is single/celibate they have that gifting and calling. If one is engaging in homosexual activity, that is defined neither as gift nor calling, but is, in every single instance in Scripture, presented as contrary to the design, not as a legitimate alternative.

That contrary activity is the sixth component: *Design Abandonment*. In Romans 1:18-20 is described how the truth of God is suppressed in unrighteousness. Verses 21-23 explains how a rejection of the Designer results in an obvious rejection of the design. Verses 24-25 identify consequence #1 – the unrighteous are given over to desires – allowed to pursue their own alternatives, since they have rejected their Creator and His design and the inherent alternative (celibacy) within His design. Verses 26-27 identify consequence #2 – the unrighteous are given over to that which is unnatural. They are allowed to take things to their logical conclusion. The Designer and the design are utterly rejected, and all that is left is the pursuit of the unnatural (that which violates the design) and the final consequence (#3) listed in 1:28 – they are given over to brokenness of mind. While God has gifted, assigned, and called humanity with marriage and some individuals with celibacy, those that have rejected Him and His design He has given over to pursue their own design along with all the associated brokenness that comes with that pursuit.

As a culminating discussion of God's design for humanity, it is obvious that there are no alternatives besides heterosexual marriage or celibacy commended or prescribed – and those two options are explicitly prescribed. Further it is evident that the homosexual "option" is presented in context not as a legitimate alternative, but as a total distortion of what God designed. Romans 1 completes the teleological cumulative case that provides certainty in Christian ethics regarding same-sex activity. To ensure that none us can boast or condemn from a perch of innocence, the context of 1:29-2:2 reiterates that we all are universally guilty, and that we have all committed acts against God that render us worthy of death. All of us like sheep have gone astray, each to his own way, but the Lord has caused the iniquity of us all to fall upon Him.[51]

While the Inherent Design View overcomes the limitations of the other two views, namely in that it (1) is more methodologically consistent with a literal grammatical-historical approach to the Scriptures, (2) draws exegetically justifiable conclusions about the character of God and the origin of morality, and (3) recognizes the progress of revelation allowing for both a cogency and discontinuity in God's revelation on the matter, there is an additional element that this writer finds compelling. This is not a device for justifying or condemning a particular lifestyle, rather it is an attempt at simply understanding what and who our Creator has designed us to be, and how we can be restored to right relationship with Him when we fail to walk as designed. God isn't a hateful Creator who has excluded those who identify as LGBTQ from intimacy and joy. On the contrary, He has put in place a design wherein we can all experience the richest of His blessings through His grace as we come to know Him and the pattern He gave to us, so that we might see His fingerprints in our lives, submit to Him as our Designer, and rejoice. It is when we encounter the profound nature of our Designer, as revealed in His design, that we can respond as prescribed with the right kind of love toward Him and toward others – love from a pure heart, a good conscience, and a sincere faith.

---

[51] Isaiah 53:6.

The Sofa Rule

15
Why I Am Not a Calvinist... Or an Arminian

While we often desire to align with particular historical theological views, it is usually the case that historical perspectives are not fully adequate in explaining the Biblical position. In the case of the Calvinism/Arminianism debate, the labels aren't even adequate in explaining the positions of the men they supposedly represent. Calvin himself actually had nothing to do with the formal five points of Calvinism, as they were actually developed through the Synod of Dort (1618-1619) in response to the teachings of followers of Jacobus Arminius.

These followers were called Remonstrants, after the document published in 1610 called the Remonstrance, which challenged the Belgic Confession (1562-1566) and some of John Calvin's and Theodore Beza's teaching. Still it is helpful to understand the theological positions, but it is far more important to understand the Biblical data on those issues. What follows is a brief synopsis, evaluating basic components of Calvinism and Arminianism in light of Biblical data.

ASSESSING CALVINISM

Calvinism is typically identified by the classic TULIP system of Total depravity, Unconditional election, Limited atonement, Irresistible grace, and Perseverance of saints.

Total Depravity

The Calvinist Position

> Man, by his fall into a state of sin, hath wholly lost all ability of will to any spiritual good accompanying salvation; so as a natural man being altogether averse from that good, and dead in sin, is not able, by his own strength, to convert himself, or to prepare himself thereunto.[1]

The Biblical Data

This statement is consistent with Romans 3:9-20, 5:1-12, and Ephesians 2:1-3 in describing our former estate. The insufficiency here is in the explanation of how man is presently in such a helpless state. Calvin advocated the idea of federal headship – that Adam was representative of all humanity in his sin. But the Biblical conception of human depravity is not simply that we are all in sin because Adam represented us. Adam's son was born in his image and likeness.[2] So the sin Adam bore is passed down to all of us as *an inherited trait*. We have the sin nature just as Adam. Insofar as all are sinners by nature,[3] we all bear the consequences of spiritual death[4] and physical

---

[1] Westminster Confession, 9:III.
[2] Genesis 4:3.
[3] Romans 5:12, Ephesians 2:3.
[4] Genesis 2:17.

death.[5] This is likely why David referred to himself as having been brought forth in iniquity and conceived in sin.[6]

In short, the Biblical concept of human depravity seems to include representation in Adam, but extends beyond that to an ontological depravity due to our own individual natures: we are born from a sinner – in the image and likeness of that sinner – therefore, we are by nature, sinners.

Unconditional Election

The Calvinist Position

> By the decree of God, for the manifestation of his glory, some men and angels are predestinated unto everlasting life, and others foreordained to everlasting death. IV. These angels and men, thus predestinated and foreordained, are particularly and unchangeably designed; and their number is so certain and definite that it can not be either increased or diminished. V. Those of mankind that are predestinated unto life, God, before the foundation of the world was laid, according to his eternal and immutable purpose, and the secret counsel and good pleasure of his will, hath chosen in Christ, unto everlasting glory, out of his free grace and love alone, without any foresight of faith or good works, or perseverance in either of them, or any other thing in the creature, as conditions, or causes moving him thereunto; and all to the praise of his glorious grace. VI. As God hath appointed the elect unto glory, so hath he, by the eternal and most free purpose of his will, foreordained all the means thereunto. Wherefore they who are elected being fallen in Adam are redeemed by Christ, are effectually called unto faith in Christ by his Spirit working in due season; are justified, adopted, sanctified, and kept by his power through faith unto salvation. Neither are any other redeemed by Christ, effectually called, justified, adopted, sanctified, and saved, but the elect only. VII. The rest of mankind, God was pleased,

---

[5] Genesis 3:19.
[6] Psalm 51:5.

according to the unsearchable counsel of his own will, whereby he extendeth or withholdeth mercy as he pleaseth, for the glory of his sovereign power over his creatures, to pass by, and to ordain them to dishonor and wrath for their sin, to the praise of his glorious justice.[7]

The Biblical Data

In these assertions there are some overstatements. Angels are predestined to eternal life? Where does the Bible assert that? Their number can be neither increased or diminished? Upon what Biblical basis? These statements are possibly true, but they go beyond what is written. There is a subtle problem here, and it is not necessarily in the conclusion of double election (that God elected believers to salvation and unbelievers to damnation). The problem is in the means of arriving at that conclusion – theological (hermeneutic) method.

To illustrate, The Canon of Dort, Rejection of Errors, First Head, Paragraph 8 quotes three passages: Romans 9:18 ("he hardens whom he wants to harden"), Matthew 13:11 ("not revealed to them"), and Matthew 11:25-26 ("you have hidden these things from the wise"). But in each of these three cases the Canon of Dort goes too far. The content of the what was hidden in Matthew 13:11 was the mysteries of the kingdom – the things Jesus was sharing with the disciples in private – the things of the kingdom, not of individual salvation. And are we to understand Matthew 11:25 as restricting saving knowledge from the wise and intelligent? If so then Paul is wrong, because he admits there are some wise who are saved.[8] The hardening of Romans 9 has nothing to do with election. In fact, the first Biblical instance of hardening is done with Pharaoh after the

---

[7] Westminster Confession, 3:III-VII.
[8] 1 Corinthians 1:26.

fact.[9] We cannot say whether Pharaoh was ever a believer or not, because the Bible doesn't reveal it. While double election seems logically possible, it is not exegetically provable. It may even be probable, but it cannot be justified as Biblical fact.

Limited Atonement

The Calvinist Position

> The death of the Son of God is the only and most perfect sacrifice and satisfaction for sin, and is of infinite worth and value, abundantly sufficient to expiate the sins of the whole world.[10]
>
> For this was the sovereign counsel and most gracious will and purpose of God the Father that the quickening and saving efficacy of the most precious death of His Son should extend to all the elect, for bestowing upon them alone the gift of justifying faith, thereby to bring them infallibly to salvation; that is, it was the will of God that Christ by the blood of the cross, whereby He confirmed the new covenant, should effectually redeem out of every people, tribe, nation, and language, all those, and those only, who were from eternity chosen to salvation and given to Him by the Father; that He should confer upon them faith, which, together with all the other saving gifts of the Holy Spirit, He purchased for them by His death; should purge them from all sin, both original and actual, whether committed before or after believing; and having faithfully preserved them even to the end, should at last bring them, free from every spot and blemish, to the enjoyment of glory in His own presence forever."[11]
>
> That God the Father has ordained His Son to the death of the cross without a certain and definite decree to save any, so that the necessity, profitableness, and worth of what Christ merited by His death might have existed, and might remain in all its parts

---

[9] Exodus 4:21.
[10] Canon of Dort, Second Head, Article 3.
[11] Canon of Dort, Second Head, Article 8.

complete, perfect, and intact, even if the merited redemption had never in fact been applied to any person."[12]

The Biblical Data

Contemporary explanations of limited atonement rest upon a basic syllogism:

P1: None of Jesus' blood was wasted
P2: His blood provided a complete satisfaction for sin wherever it is efficacious
C: Jesus could only have died for the elect, who would ultimately receive redemption

Interestingly, this syllogism is not found explicitly in Calvin's writings, in the Canons of Dort, or in the Westminster Confession. However the Dort statement (Rejection of Errors, 2:1) provides the logical basis for it: *only the elect can be saved, and Christ's death would have been wasted if never applied to any person*. This Dort statement assumes the necessity of unconditional election, and undergirds the efficacy of the atonement upon that principle.

In short, if Jesus paid the price for the sin of those who wouldn't believe, then His blood was wasted. The Belgic Confession[13] illustrates the significance of this: "Therefore, for any to assert, that Christ is not sufficient, but that something more is required besides him, would be too gross a blasphemy: for hence it would follow that Christ was but half a Savior."

The logic is not too difficult to follow, and if the premises are correct, then the conclusion is also correct. However, that Jesus did die to pay the penalty for all (elect or not) is clearly

---

[12] Rejection of Errors, 2:1.
[13] Article XXII.

stated in 1 John 2:2 – "and He Himself is the propitiation for our sins; and not for ours only, but also for those of the whole world." This simply stated passage underscores the fact that the limited atonement view is not accurate. It is better to understand Christ's sacrifice through the lens of the Passover illustration. The blood shed by the lambs was perfectly efficacious blood, but it had to be applied in a specific manner, otherwise it did not provide benefit for the individual.[14] The only way to justify the limited atonement view is to change the meaning of the words in 1 John 2:2, *and that is simply not allowed by the literal grammatical-historical hermeneutic.*

Irresistible Grace

The Calvinist Position

> That some receive the gift of faith from God, and others do not receive it, proceeds from God's eternal decree. "For known unto God are all his works from the beginning of the world" (Acts 15:18). "who works out everything in conformity with the purpose of his will" (Eph 1:11). According to which decree He graciously softens the hearts of the elect, however obstinate, and inclines them to believe; while He leaves the non-elect in His just judgment to their own wickedness and obduracy. And herein is especially displayed the profound, the merciful, and at the same time the righteous discrimination between men equally involved in ruin; or that decree of election and reprobation, revealed in the Word of God, which, though men of perverse, impure, and unstable minds wrest it to their own destruction, yet to holy and pious souls affords unspeakable consolation.[15]
>
> This purpose proceeding from everlasting love towards the elect, has from the beginning of the world to this day been powerfully

---

[14] Exodus 12:7,13.
[15] Canon of Dort, First Head, Article 6.

accomplished, and will henceforward still continue to be accomplished, notwithstanding all the ineffectual opposition of the gates of hell, so that the elect in due time may be gathered together into one, and that there may never be wanting a church composed of believers, the foundation of which is laid in the blood of Christ, which may steadfastly love, and faithfully serve him as their Savior, who as a bridegroom for his bride, laid down his life for them upon the cross, and which may celebrate his praises here and through all eternity.[16]

The Biblical Data

In my estimation, this is probably the best (most Biblically) stated of the five points. This point reflects accurately the process described in Romans 8:28-30, that the foreknowledge of God with respect to the ones He predestines and calls and justifies concludes with their glorification. The Dort statements logically presuppose double election, and I have already addressed the exegetical challenge there: while logically possible, it is not exegetically certain. These Dort statements of irresistible grace come close to what is Biblically certain, with only the subtle extension beyond what is written.

Perseverance of Saints

The Calvinist Position

> And as God Himself is most wise, unchangeable, omniscient, and omnipotent, so the election made by Him can neither be interrupted nor changed, recalled, or annulled; neither can the elect be cast away, nor their number diminished."[17]
>
> May not true believers, by reason of their imperfections, and the many temptations and sins they are overtaken with, fall away

---

[16] Canon of Dort, Second Head, Article 9.
[17] Canon of Dort, First Head, Article 11.

from a state of grace? True believers, by reason of the unchangeable love of God, and His decree and covenant to give them perseverance, their inseparable union with Christ, His continual intercession for them, and the Spirit and seed of God abiding in them, can neither totally nor finally fall away from the state of grace, but are kept by the power of God through faith unto salvation.[18]

The Biblical Data

The Dort statement appeals to election, while the Westminster statement appeals to God's giving of perseverance. The conclusion that believers are eternally secure is Biblically accurate, but the means of arriving at that conclusion is better connected to (1) the present tense possession of eternal life by the believer in Jesus Christ,[19] and (2) the protection of God.[20] In 1 Peter 1:3-5, for example, there are eleven statements affirming the security of the believer, and none of them depend on or are focused on the believer, but all are focused on God's activity. The issue here is that the phrase *perseverance of saints* implies some activity on the part of the believer, whereas the Biblical data is explicitly theocentric regarding God as exclusive Protector.

ASSESSING ARMINIANISM

The *Remonstrance* of 1610, by followers of Jacobus Arminius, counters five points of doctrine that were understood to be Calvinistic teachings. The *Remonstrance* first denies the five Calvinistic tenets, and then positively asserts five articles of doctrine that present a completely different idea of God's character than does Calvinism.

---

[18] Westminster Larger Catechism, Q&A 79.
[19] John 6:47.
[20] 1 Peter 1:5.

Conditional Predestination

The Arminian Position

> God has immutably decreed, from eternity, to save those men who, by the grace of the Holy Spirit, believe in Jesus Christ, and by the same grace persevere in the obedience of faith to the end; and, on the other hand, to condemn the unbelievers and unconverted (John iii. 36). Election and condemnation are thus conditioned by foreknowledge, and made dependent on the foreseen faith or unbelief of men."[21]

The Biblical Data

The first phrase of Article I illustrates the primary challenge of the entire Calvinism/Arminianism debate: "God has immutably decreed, from eternity..." This isn't necessarily a false statement, but it isn't grounded exegetically. Upon what basis can we say *when* God made such determinations, other than before the foundation of the world?[22] The lack of precision here lends opportunity for the further development of such constructs as the covenant of redemption and the lapsarian/superlapsarian/supralapsarian perspectives – none of which have any actual exegetical grounding. This particular statement goes just a little further than what is written. The basis of authority for the entire discussion has historically been theological constructs, rather than exegetically precise statements.

Further, the statement describes how saints "persevere in the obedience of faith" as a necessary prerequisite to salvation, making salvation a strictly future thing conditioned

---

[21] Remonstrance, Article I.
[22] Ephesians 1:4.

upon perseverance. But the obedience of faith in John 3:36 is not referring to obedience that comes after faith, but rather having faith as obedience. The only imperative for unbelievers is to believe in him,[23] thus the obedience discussed in 3:36 is synonymous with belief, and not an additional condition. By the subtle misinterpretation of faith and obedience as two separate things, the Remonstrance makes salvation a conditional reward that can be lost at any point. The article also fails to acknowledge that eternal life is a present tense possession of the believer,[24] and thus cannot be conditioned on future actions.

The final statement on election and condemnation as conditioned by foreknowledge also goes beyond what is written. Ephesians 1:5 implies that the predestining is based solely on His will, whereas Arminian thought would understand the predestination of Romans 8:29 as an effect of the cause that is foreknowledge. Consequently, in Arminianism, God does not predestine from His strength, but only from His knowledge. Thus from an Arminian perspective, His sovereign control is limited.

Universal Atonement

The Arminian Position

> Christ, the Saviour of the world, died for all men and for every man, and his grace is extended to all. His atoning sacrifice is in and of itself sufficient for the redemption of the whole world, and is intended for all by God the Father. But its inherent sufficiency does not necessarily imply its actual efficiency. The grace of God may be resisted, and only those who accept it by faith are actually

---

[23] John 3:16.
[24] 6:47.

saved. He who is lost, is lost by his own guilt (John iii. 16; 1 John ii. 2). The Arminians agree with the orthodox in holding the doctrine of a vicarious or expiatory atonement, in opposition to the Socinians; but they soften it down, and represent its direct effect to be to enable God, consistently with his justice and veracity, to enter into a new covenant with men, under which pardon is conveyed to all men on condition of repentance and faith. The immediate effect of Christ's death was not the salvation, but only the salvability of sinners by the removal of the legal obstacles, and opening the door for pardon and reconciliation. They reject the doctrine of a limited atonement, which is connected with the supralapsarian view of predestination, but is disowned by moderate Calvinists, who differ from the Arminians in all other points. Calvin himself says that Christ died sufficienter pro omnibus, efficaciter pro electis."[25]

The Biblical Data

The first statement here regarding the extent, sufficiency, and efficiency of the atonement is actually a very good one, exegetically defensible from the two passages cited.[26] Jesus died for all a sufficient death, but just as the blood of the Passover lamb had to be applied in order to be efficient (or in order to actually save[27]), so the blood of Jesus must be applied through belief in Him. The statement goes too far, however, in asserting that God enters into a new covenant with all men. There is no exegetical data supporting, for example, the church being brought into a covenant relationship.

---

[25] Remonstrance, Article II.
[26] John 3:16, 1 John 2:2.
[27] Exodus 12:7.

Saving Faith

The Arminian Position

> Man in his fallen state is unable to accomplish any thing really and truly good, and therefore also unable to attain to saving faith, unless he be regenerated and renewed by God in Christ through the Holy Spirit (John xv. 5)."[28]

The Biblical Data

Supporting the statement that regeneration precedes faith, the Remonstrance cites John 15:5, which has nothing whatsoever to do with saving faith – in fact, Jesus' statement in that passage is addressed to eleven men who Jesus says already have saving faith.[29] This is exegetically bizarre, and is no less logically odd. To illustrate, imagine a man walking on the side of a highway. He is pondering his sin and what God has done for him. In the Arminian model, in a moment in time he is regenerated, and a split second later – as a result of that regeneration – is about to have saving faith. But in that nano second (or whatever period of time elapses) between the regeneration and the act of faith, the man is struck by a car and dies immediately. By definition, he would have been regenerated apart from faith. Regeneration preceding faith is not exegetically or logically plausible.[30] Some degree of divine enablement allowing saving faith is clearly in view,[31] but regeneration goes much too far.

---

[28] Remonstrance, Article III.
[29] John 15:3.
[30] See Chapter 17, "No Time for Salvation" for an expansion on this discussion.
[31] E.g., John 6:44.

Irresistible Grace

The Arminian Position

> Grace is the beginning, continuation, and end of our spiritual life, so that man can neither think nor do any good or resist sin without prevening, co-operating, and assisting grace. But as for the manner of co-operation, this grace is not irresistible, for many resist the Holy Ghost (Acts vii.)."[32]

The Biblical Data

This statement attempts to accommodate the false dichotomy that either God is sovereign and no one can resist Him at all, or He is not sovereignly in control, and because of that He can be resisted. The cited martyr of Stephen illustrates a resistance to God's word, but gives no commentary supporting any lack of control on God's part. Notice how this statement is logically grounded on the final statement of the first article – that God's sovereignty is expressed as a result of foreknowledge, and not the other way around. Arminianism says He decrees it because He knows it. Calvinism says He knows it because He decrees it. But what does the Bible say? Ephesians 1:5 is clear regarding cause and effect, whereas Romans 8:29 is not considering cause and effect at all.

Uncertainty of Perseverance

The Arminian Position

> Although grace is sufficient and abundant to preserve the faithful through all trials and temptations for life everlasting, it has not

---

[32] Remonstrance, Article IV.

yet been proved from the Scriptures that grace, once given, can never be lost. On this point the disciples of Arminius went further, and taught the possibility of a total and final fall of believers from grace. They appealed to such passages where believers are warned against this very danger, and to such examples as Solomon and Judas. They moreover denied, with the Roman Catholics, that any body can have a certainty of salvation except by special revelation. These five points the Remonstrants declare to be in harmony with the Word of God, edifying and, as far as they go, sufficient for salvation. They protest against the charge of changing the Christian Reformed religion, and claim toleration and legal protection for their doctrine.[33]

The Biblical Data

The first paragraph of this statement is incompatible with the assertion of John 6:47 that at the moment of belief we possess eternal life, which by definition, cannot be lost. 1 Peter 1:3-5 contains no less than eleven statements affirming the eternal security of the believer. Romans 8:1 says there is no condemnation for those in Christ. How can those in Christ ever undergo the condemnation of being cast out if there is no condemnation for them? Romans 8:29-30 says that God's foreknowledge and predestination is just as true of the believer as is being called, justified, and glorified – the outcome is certain. Romans 8:39 says that no created thing can separate us from the love of God.

Further, the appeals to Solomon and Judas don't support the Remonstrance's argument here. We have no timeline of Solomon's sin with respect to when he authored Ecclesiastes. However, it appears that Ecclesiastes was written as a final explanation of the journey he had taken, and that his *conclusion*

---

[33] Remonstrance, Article V.

affirms the fear of the Lord.[34] Judas was a scoundrel[35] whose betrayal of Christ was consistent with his inner character, and yet who was remorseful after the betrayal.[36] He didn't fall from grace. If anything, we can hope he came to know the depths of God's grace *after* his great sin. Further, Judas' betrayal was apparently facilitated by some degree of possession of Judas by Satan.[37] Should we understand that all who are under grace are in potential danger of Satanic possession, and that we all must be on guard against such a danger? There is no exegetical data supporting that.

Finally, the concluding statement that the five points constructed by the Remonstrants are in harmony with the word of God is evidently not true when the five points are considered against the light of Scripture. Certainly there is some Biblical truth interspersed throughout the five points (especially in the second point). But insofar as they rely on theological suppositions and constructs rather than exegetical ones, there is some dissonance with the Biblical data.

A THIRD OPTION

The Calvinism/Arminianism debate considers three essential issues: (1) The degree of God's activity in human salvation, (2) the degree of human culpability, and (3) the degree of human activity in salvation. Historically Calvin placed strongest emphasis on God's activity in salvation, whereas Arminius tended towards emphasizing human volition over God's volition. Ultimately the two theological traditions are

---

[34] Ecclesiastes 11:9, 12:1, 12:13-14.
[35] John 12:6.
[36] Matthew 27:3.
[37] Luke 22:3, John 13:2.

trying to resolve an apparent conflict between God's sovereignty and human responsibility, and they both attempt resolution by means of extra-Biblical rationalistic constructs.

I suggest it is due to the artificial nature of these arguments that there has been no historical resolution to the debate. Because the base of authority for both sides is subjective (rationalistic theology) rather than objective (exegesis), neither side can, in my estimation, claim the full authority of Scripture. Hence, the longstanding and unresolved debate.

In 1 Corinthians 4:6, Paul expresses his desire that the Corinthians "learn not to exceed what is written, so that no one of you will become arrogant in behalf of one against the other." In order to maintain the proper humility (and to ensure the highest degree of accuracy), it is best when dealing with the mysteries of God[38] not to expand their definitions beyond what God has revealed. This is an important principle broadly applicable throughout the Christian life, and certainly in resolving any theological difficulty.

Preferring an exegetical approach to a rationalistic one, we should be willing to endure some uncertainty in theological conclusions where the Bible does not address certain details, rather than to demand a theology that answers every detailed inquiry but which is not grounded on the certainty of revelation. In other words, where the Bible is silent, we simply cannot extrapolate authoritative conclusions. Still we are left with the question: if neither Calvinism nor Arminianism is sufficient in representing the Biblical data, then what is a more sufficient explanation?

---

[38] 1 Corinthians 4:1.

The following series of seven Biblical assertions may be helpful in clarifying the issue. These assertions address key components of both the Calvinist and Arminian perspectives, and offer an alternative explanation of God's character and working:

>Assertion #1: The Biblical God exists and He is holy.
>Assertion #2: He has revealed Himself authoritatively.
>Assertion #3: He has described the human condition as universally fallen.
>Assertion #4: He engages the human condition based on His own will.
>Assertion #5: His salvation is legitimately provided for and offered to all.
>Assertion #6: He is sovereign over human response and still holds humanity responsible.
>Assertion #7: There is no conflict between God's sovereignty and human responsibility.

Assertions #1 and #2 provide foundational data to address the questions. Assertion #3 answers the Calvinistic concept of total depravity. Assertion #4 answers the Calvinistic concept of unconditional election and the Arminian concept of conditional predestination. Assertion #5 answers the Calvinistic concept of limited atonement and the Arminian concepts of universal atonement and saving faith. Assertion #6 answers the Calvinistic concepts of irresistible grace and perseverance of saints, and the Arminian concepts of resistible grace and uncertainty of perseverance. Assertion #7 answers the rationalistic premise that seems to provide the philosophical undergirding for the entire Calvinism/Arminianism debate.

#1 The Biblical God Exists, and He is Holy

"In the beginning God..." – Genesis 1:1. "In the beginning was the Word, and the Word was with God, and the Word was God. He was in the beginning with God. All things came into being through Him, and apart from Him nothing came into being that has come into being" – John 1:1-3. "...and the Spirit of God was moving over the surface of the waters" – Genesis 1:3. "Listen to Me, O Jacob, even Israel whom I called; I am He, I am the first, I am also the last...And now the Lord GOD has sent Me, and His Spirit" – Isaiah 48:11, 16. "Holy, Holy, Holy, is the LORD of hosts, The whole earth is full of His glory" – Isaiah 6:3. "HOLY, HOLY, HOLY *is* THE LORD GOD, THE ALMIGHTY, WHO WAS AND WHO IS AND WHO IS TO COME" – Revelation 4:7.

#2 He Has Revealed Himself Authoritatively

"Then God said..." – Genesis 1:3. "...that which is known about God is evident within them; for God made it evident to them. For since the creation of the world His invisible attributes, His eternal power and divine nature, have been clearly seen, being understood through what has been made, so that they are without excuse" – Romans 1:19-20. "God, after He spoke long ago to the fathers in the prophets in many portions and in many ways, in these last days has spoken to us in His Son, whom He appointed heir of all things, through whom also He made the world" – Hebrews 1:1-2. "No one has seen God at any time; the only begotten one (*monogenes*) who is God, in the bosom of the Father, He has explained Him" – John 1:18. "All Scripture is inspired by God and profitable for teaching, for reproof, for correction, for training in righteousness; so that the man of God may be adequate, equipped for every good work" – 2 Timothy 3:16-17. "But know this first of all, that no prophecy of Scripture is *a matter* of one's own interpretation, for no prophecy was ever made by an act of human will, but men moved by the Holy Spirit spoke from God" – 2 Peter 1:20-21. "For I am not ashamed of the gospel, for it is the power of God for salvation to everyone who believes, to the Jew first and also to the Greek. For in it *the* righteousness of God is revealed from faith to faith; as it is written, "BUT THE RIGHTEOUS *man* SHALL LIVE BY FAITH"" – Romans 1:16-17.

#3 He Has Described the Human Condition as Universally Fallen

The descendants of Adam did not choose to be born, and yet we are all held accountable for his sin – we are all condemned. The human condition was not chosen by anyone after Adam, yet we prove we are in Adam's likeness and image by adding our own sin.

"For in the day that you eat from it you will surely die" – Genesis 2:17. "...she took from its fruit and ate; and she gave also to her husband with her, and he ate" – Genesis 3:6. "When Adam had lived one hundred and thirty years, he became the father of *a son* in his own likeness, according to his image..." – Genesis 5:3. "Then the LORD saw that the wickedness of man was great on the earth, and that every intent of the thoughts of his heart was only evil continually" – Genesis 6:5. "Through one man sin entered into the world, and death through sin, and so death spread to all men, because all sinned...by the transgression of the one the many died...through one transgression there resulted condemnation to all men..." – Romans 5:12, 15, 18. "For all of us have become like one who is unclean, And all our righteous deeds are like a filthy garment; And all of us wither like a leaf, And our iniquities, like the wind, take us away" – Isaiah 64:6. "Both Jews and Greeks are all under sin… as it is written, THERE IS NONE RIGHTEOUS, NOT EVEN ONE; THERE IS NONE WHO UNDERSTANDS, THERE IS NONE WHO SEEKS FOR GOD; ALL HAVE TURNED ASIDE, TOGETHER THEY HAVE BECOME USELESS; THERE IS NONE WHO DOES GOOD, THERE IS NOT EVEN ONE" – Romans 3:9-12.

#4 He Engages the Human Condition, Based on His Own Will

The Father chose, foreknew, and predestined. There is no order of process identified here, only statements that He is the accomplisher of these processes.

"For He says to Moses, "I WILL HAVE MERCY ON WHOM I HAVE MERCY, AND I WILL HAVE COMPASSION ON WHOM I HAVE COMPASSION." So then it *does* not *depend* on the man who wills or the man who runs, but on God who has mercy. For the Scripture says to Pharaoh, "FOR THIS VERY PURPOSE I RAISED YOU UP, TO DEMONSTRATE MY POWER IN YOU, AND THAT MY NAME MIGHT BE PROCLAIMED THROUGHOUT THE WHOLE EARTH." So then He has mercy on whom He desires, and He hardens whom He desires" – Romans 9:15-18. "All things have been handed over to Me by My Father; and no one knows the Son except the Father; nor does anyone know the Father except the Son, and anyone to whom the Son wills to reveal *Him*" – Matthew 11:27. "…just as He chose us in Him before the foundation of the world, that we would be holy and blameless before Him. In love He predestined us to adoption as sons through Jesus Christ to Himself, according to the kind intention of His will, to the praise of the glory of His grace, which He freely bestowed on us in the Beloved" – Ephesians 1:4-6. "For those whom He foreknew, He also predestined *to become* conformed to the image of His Son, so that He would be the firstborn among many brethren; and these whom He predestined, He also called; and these whom He called, He also justified; and these whom He justified, He also glorified" – Romans 8:29-30.

#5 His Salvation is Legitimately Provided for and Offered to All

The Son died as a Substitute for all. His death accomplished everything necessary for the salvation of everyone, except for personal application through belief.

"We have fixed our hope on the living God, who is the Savior of all men, especially of believers" – 1 Timothy 4:10. "And He Himself is the propitiation for our sins; and not for ours only, but also for *those of* the whole world" – 1 John 2:2. "The Father draws: No one can come to Me unless the Father who sent Me draws him; and I will raise him up on the last day" – John 6:44. "The Spirit convicts the world: And He, when He comes, will convict the world concerning sin and righteousness and judgment; concerning sin, because they do not believe in Me" – John 16:8-9. The Son redeems. As we are purchased with His blood, if He has indeed paid for all sin, then there is now no condemnation for those in Christ Jesus.[39] In other words, by virtue of His blood, those who believe in Him are eternally secure. "In Him we have redemption through His blood, the forgiveness of our trespasses, according to the riches of His grace" – Ephesians 1:7.

Faith and regeneration are concurrent, not subsequent. There is no cause and effect time stamp discussed in Ephesians 2:5-9 that would justify either the belief that saving faith occurs at a time before regeneration takes place, or that regeneration precedes faith in order to make faith possible. Instead, belief and

---

[39] Romans 8:1.

life are generally spoken of as concurrent happenings.[40] "Even when we were dead in our transgressions, made us alive together with Christ (by grace you have been saved)...For by grace you have been saved through faith; and that not of yourselves, *it is* the gift of God" – Ephesians 2:5,8.

The Spirit seals. The Spirit's sealing is a pledge, or down payment, and underscores the certainty of our ultimate salvation. This is not perseverance of saints, but rather preservation of saints. "In Him, you also, after listening to the message of truth, the gospel of your salvation—having also believed, you were sealed in Him with the Holy Spirit of promise, who is given as a pledge of our inheritance, with a view to the redemption of *God's own* possession, to the praise of His glory" – Ephesians 1:13-14.

The Father conforms believers to the image of Christ. "For those whom He foreknew, He also predestined to become conformed to the image of His Son, so that He would be the firstborn among many brethren; and these whom He predestined, He also called; and these whom He called, He also justified; and these whom He justified, He also glorified" – Romans 8:29-30.

#6 He Is Sovereign Over Human Response, and Still Holds Humanity Accountable

Though God accomplishes the salvific work on His own, He demands that individuals believe in Him, and holds them accountable if they don't. And whether or not we believe is within the sphere of His sovereignty (as is everything). "For God so loved the world, that He gave His only begotten Son, that the

---

[40] E.g., John 6:47.

believing one in Him shall not perish, but have eternal life" – John 3:16.

The personal application of salvation is conditioned upon belief. Once the belief is there, eternal life is there, in the present tense. One cannot possess eternal life at the moment of belief, if he could ever lose it at any point in the future (otherwise, it would not be eternal, but rather temporary). "Truly, truly, I say to you, the believing one has eternal life" – John 6:47. "For He says to Moses, "I WILL HAVE MERCY ON WHOM I HAVE MERCY, AND I WILL HAVE COMPASSION ON WHOM I HAVE COMPASSION." So then it *does* not *depend* on the man who wills or the man who runs, but on God who has mercy. For the Scripture says to Pharaoh, "FOR THIS VERY PURPOSE I RAISED YOU UP, TO DEMONSTRATE MY POWER IN YOU, AND THAT MY NAME MIGHT BE PROCLAIMED THROUGHOUT THE WHOLE EARTH." So then He has mercy on whom He desires, and He hardens whom He desires" – Romans 9:15-18. "Or does not the potter have a right over the clay, to make from the same lump one vessel for honorable use and another for common use? What if God, although willing to demonstrate His wrath and to make His power known, endured with much patience vessels of wrath prepared for destruction? And *He did so* to make known the riches of His glory upon vessels of mercy, which He prepared beforehand for glory, *even* us, whom He also called, not from among Jews only, but also from among Gentiles" – Romans 9:22-24. "...and I give eternal life to them, and they will never perish; and no one will snatch them out of My hand. My Father, who has given *them* to Me, is greater than all; and no one is able to snatch *them* out of the Father's hand" – John 10:28-29.

He does not desire that any should perish. "The Lord is not slow about His promise, as some count slowness, but is patient toward you, not wishing for any to perish but for all to come to repentance" – 2 Peter 3:9. Nonetheless, some do perish. "And if anyone's name was not found written in the book of life, he was thrown into the lake of fire" – Revelation 20:15.

While there is no Biblical explanation for how these two seemingly paradoxical premises can both be true, the Bible asserts them both. Rather than redefine either premise to soften or strengthen their meaning, it is better (more exegetically justifiable) to allow the two statements to stand on their own, and for us to recognize that God is the one determining what He wants and what He will get, and as Sovereign, He is the one determining what is possible and what is not. It is therefore possible for one to resist His desire or will in some respects,[41] though it is not possible to resist His will in others.[42] The Bible never explicitly discusses the difference, so any discussion on this point is merely speculative.

#7 There Is No Conflict Between God's Sovereignty and Human Responsibility

"For My thoughts are not your thoughts, Nor are your ways My ways," declares the LORD. "For *as* the heavens are higher than the earth, So are My ways higher than your ways And My thoughts than your thoughts" – Isaiah 55:8-9. "Oh, the depth of the riches both of the wisdom and knowledge of God! How unsearchable are His judgments and unfathomable His ways! For WHO HAS KNOWN THE MIND OF THE LORD, OR WHO BECAME HIS COUNSELOR? Or WHO HAS FIRST GIVEN TO HIM THAT IT MIGHT BE PAID BACK TO HIM AGAIN? For from Him and through Him and to Him are all things. To Him *be* the glory forever.

---

[41] As in βουλόμενός, 2 Peter 3:9
[42] βουλήματι, Romans 9:19.

Amen" – Romans 11:33-36. "But now, O LORD, You are our Father, We are the clay, and You our potter; And all of us are the work of Your hand" – Isaiah 64:8. "Woe to *the one* who quarrels with his Maker – An earthenware vessel among the vessels of earth! Will the clay say to the potter, 'What are you doing?' Or the thing you are making *say,* 'He has no hands'" – Isaiah 45:9.

Conclusion

The premise that God cannot hold His creation accountable for something it did not choose is not an exegetically defensible premise (whether His creation chose or not is irrelevant to this point). Just as the potter has authority over the clay, God has authority over His creation to hold it accountable for whatever He wishes to hold it accountable. He is not caught in any contradiction for doing so. If we don't like that He is sovereign and still holds His creation accountable, then that is a problem with our submission, not with His justice or righteousness.

16
Does Grace Extend to Everyone?[1]

A literal translation of 1 John 2:2 reads as follows: "And He a propitiation He is for the sins of us, not for those of us only, but also for those of the whole world." At first glance the verse seems simple enough, but there has historically been startling disagreement regarding its intended meaning. John MacArthur concludes that the passage cannot mean that Jesus paid for the sins of the whole world, insisting that, "Jesus didn't pay for the sins of Judas…or Adolf Hitler."[2] MacArthur supports his view with an appeal to John 11:52,[3] which he says indicates that Jesus died only for the children of God. The passage reads, "…and not for the nation only, but in order that He might also gather together into one the children of God who are scattered abroad."[4] John Piper's explanation of the passage is similar, as

---

[1] Presented to the 2015 FGA National Conference, Arlington, Texas, October 13, 2015.
[2] John Macarthur, "Limited Atonement: Explained – 1 John 2:2" https://www.youtube.com/watch?v=DepxyWF8euA.
[3] "…And not for the nation only, but in order that He might also gather together into one the children of God who are scattered abroad."
[4] NASB.

he, like MacArthur, supports his 1 John 2:2 interpretation from an appeal to John 11:52.[5] R.C. Sproul explains 1 John 2:2 as follows: "He is the "propitiation" for us, the one who endured the wrath we deserve so that divine justice is fulfilled, not set aside. Christ is the propitiation for "the whole world," not because He made atonement for every sinner, but because He redeemed not only Jews but people *from all parts of the world*' [emphasis mine].[6]

How can a verse so seemingly simple be construed to say almost the opposite of what it seems intended to say? To put it simply, there is theological turf at stake. If the literal translation (that Christ is the propitiation for the whole world) reflects the intended meaning, then the Reformed doctrine of limited atonement collapses, and with it, the other four points of Calvinism as understood by contemporary Reformed thinkers. Note Sproul's recognition that, "if a person really understands the other four points and is thinking at all clearly, he must believe in limited atonement because of what Martin Luther called a resistless logic."[7]

But what if limited atonement is debunked by 1 John 2:2 (or other passages)? Sproul makes a telling admission: "I don't think we want to believe in a God who sends Christ to die on the cross and then crosses His fingers, hoping that someone will

---

[5] John Piper, "John Piper on Limited Atonement" https://www.youtube.com/watch?v=tZEIPPgMkFA.
[6] R.C. Sproul, "Our Righteous Advocate," Ligonier Ministries at http://www.ligonier.org/learn/devotionals/our-righteous-advocate/.
[7] R.C. Sproul, *The Truth of the Cross* (Lake Mary, FL: Reformation Trust Publishing, 2007), 142.

take advantage of that atoning death."[8] *I don't think we want to believe...*

The Reformed Doctrine of Limited Atonement

In order to understand why Sproul might make such a statement, let's examine some basics of the Reformed doctrine of limited atonement. The essential premise of the doctrine is that *the atonement is sufficient for all men, but efficient only for the elect*. On its face that doesn't sound too problematic, but the problem becomes evident when we consider what is meant by the term *efficient*. Sproul explains it this way: "It wasn't just a hypothetical atonement, it was an actual atonement. He didn't offer a hypothetical expiation for the sins of His people; their sins *were* expiated."[9]

Piper's conclusion is similar. He asserts, "When Jesus died on the cross, paying the price for us...He decisively accomplished that for His own. His sheep. His elect...He didn't just make it accomplishable. He accomplished it."[10] From this understanding, Piper considers the term *triumphantly effective atonement* as preferable to the more traditional *limited atonement*.[11] Sproul likewise re-labels the term. He says, "I prefer not to use the term limited atonement because it is misleading. I rather speak of definite redemption or definite atonement, which communicates that God the Father designed

---

[8] R.C. Sproul, "TULIP and Reformed Theology: Limited Atonement," Ligonier Ministries, November 19, 2012 at http://www.ligonier.org/blog/tulip-and-reformed-theology-limited-atonement/.
[9] Sproul, *The Truth of the Cross*, 150.
[10] John Piper, "John Piper on Limited Atonement" https://www.youtube.com/watch?v=tZEIPPgMkFA.
[11] Ibid.

the work of redemption specifically with a view to providing salvation for the elect, and that Christ died for His sheep and laid down His life for those the Father had given to Him."[12] This redefinition helps explain why the Reformed view demands that regeneration precedes faith – because in this perspective *salvation for the elect was accomplished at the cross, and not when the elect actually believed.*

Further, notice the distinction Sproul suggests between meritorious and full value of the atonement: "…its meritorious value is sufficient to cover the sins of all people, and certainly anyone who puts his or her trust in Jesus Christ will receive the full measure of the benefits of that atonement."[13] The full value is conditioned upon trust or belief. But Sproul adds another subtle yet important condition: "…the gospel is offered universally to all who are within earshot of the preaching of it, but it's not universally offered in the sense that it's offered to anyone without any conditions. It's offered to anyone who believes. It's offered to anyone who repents. Obviously the merit of the atonement of Christ is given to all who believe *and to all who repent of their sins*" [emphasis mine].[14]

It is noteworthy that Sproul views the merit of the atonement as conditional based on repentance of sins, because never in the Bible is there such a condition identified. Fifty-six times in the NT repentance is mentioned. In eight instances the NT refers to repentance *that leads to* the forgiveness of sins.[15] There are five instances in Revelation, one referring to

---

[12] Sproul, "TULIP and Reformed Theology: Limited Atonement."
[13] Ibid.
[14] Ibid.
[15] Mk 1:4, Lk 3:3, 17:3,4, 24:47, Acts 2:38, 3:19, 5:31, 2 Cor 12:21.

"Jezebel,"[16] and the others to unbelievers who have not repented of similar deeds.[17]

The only other context connecting repentance and sin is 2 Corinthians 12:21, in which Paul describes mourning for *believers* who have not repented of their impurity, immorality, and sensuality. Repentance *from* sins is simply not a Biblical condition for salvation. But what about 1 John 2:2? Does that passage refute or support the Reformed doctrine of limited atonement? We cannot dismiss the passage by referring to a distant and unconnected context, nor by quoting a catechism or creed, nor by repeating a theological supposition. We can only answer the question by exegeting the passage itself.

An Exegesis of 1 John 2:2

To adequately handle any passage we must work through some important exegetical steps. We need to (1) verify the text and translation, (2) identify background and context, (3) identify structural keys, (4) identify grammatical and syntactical keys, (5) identify lexical keys, (6) address Biblical context, and (7) consider theological context. Then we would verify our work, put it into practice in our own lives as appropriate, and communicate it with others as God gives us opportunity.[18]

---

[16] Rev 2:21.
[17] Rev 2:22, 9:20,21, 16:11.
[18] More detail is offered on these steps, and two additional steps for Bible study (secondary verification, and exposition) in Christopher Cone, *Integrating Exegesis and Exposition: Biblical Communication for Transformative Learning* (Fort Worth, TX: Exegetica Publicaitons, 2015).

(1) Text and Translation

καὶ αὐτὸς ἱλασμός ἐστιν περὶ τῶν ἁμαρτιῶν ἡμῶν, οὐ περὶ τῶν ἡμετέρων δὲ μόνον ἀλλὰ καὶ περὶ ὅλου τοῦ κόσμου.[19] A literal translation would read, "And He a propitiation He is for the sins of us, not for those of us only, but also for those of the whole world." The NASB translates the concluding phrase as "but also for those of the whole world." The ESV renders it, "but also for the sins of the whole world." The NASB italicizes the phrase *for those of,* in acknowledgment that the phrase is not actually in the Greek, but the genitive *tou kosmou* implies the phrase, so it is a sound rendering. The implication of the translation is that the propitiation is for the *sins* of the whole world, rather than being for the whole world itself.

There are a couple of minor textual variants that do not affect the meaning of the words individually or the passage as a whole. A few manuscripts read *huper ton,* rather than *peri ton.* A few spell *monon* with the omega rather than the *omicron* (the *omega* indicates the genitive plural, the *omicron* indicates the adverb or adjective). We can be confident that the English translations above are good representations of the Greek text.

(2) Background and Context

John's first epistle functions as a sequel to his Gospel. It is closely related in terminology and in thought. John addresses his letter to those he calls his little children (2:1), beloved (2:7), fathers (2:13), young men (2:13), and brethren (3:13). John writes his Gospel so that "you may believe that Jesus is the Christ, and that believing you may have life in His name" (Jn 20:31). In his first follow-up letter, John has several purposes in

---

[19] Barbara Aland et al., *The Greek New Testament*, 4th ed. (Federal Republic of Germany: United Bible Societies, 1993), 1 Jn 2:2.

mind. He proclaims "what was" so that believers might have horizontal and vertical fellowship (1:3), he writes so that his joy might be complete (1 Jn 1:4), so that his little children might not sin (1 Jn 2:1), and so that those who believe can know that they have eternal life (1 Jn 5:13). His last stated purpose builds on the purpose of John's Gospel, written so that people might believe, whereas his letter was written so that those who believe might know. In the letter, John concentrates on the vertical relationship with God, through Christ, in chapters one through three, specifically focusing on the fruit of salvation: love (2:9-10). In chapters four and five he discusses the horizontal relationship of believers to each other and underscores success in those relationships as further practical evidence of the positional reality of salvation.

(3) Structural Keys

As John's is a very personal letter, it is not structured as identifiably as is his Gospel. The thought transitions are often represented by personal address (such as in 2:1, 7, 12, 4:7, 5:13). Other times we recognize the theme shifts by transitional terms, such as *for* (*hoti*, 3:11), and thematic chiasm (as in 1:6-7, 2:9-10). John also uses imperatives to move from one theme to the next (as in 2:15, 24, 3:1, 4:1). Sometimes the topic changes are thematically self-explanatory. In any case, considering these structural keys, the letter can be outlined as follows:

    1-3 Vertical Fellowship
        1:1-4 The Basis: The Word of Life
        1:5-10 The Conditions
        2:1-2 The Advocate: Jesus Christ
        2:3-6 The Obedience

2:7-11 The Commandment: Love
2:12-14 The Maturity
2:15-17 The Warning of Worldliness
2:18-23 The Lie vs. The Truth
2:24-29 The Promise: Eternal Life
3:1-10 The Righteousness
3:11-18 The Love Needed
4-5 Horizontal Fellowship
4:1-6 The Discernment
4:7-18 The Love Explained
4:19-21 The Basis of Love
5:1-5 The Belief
5:6-12 The Witness
5:13-15 The Assurance
5:16-21 The Sin

(4) Grammatical and Syntactical Keys

The subject is *He* (*autos*), the verb is *is* (*estin*), the object is *propitiation* (*hilasmos*). The third person singular pronoun (*autos*) along with the third person singular verb (*estin*) emphasize that it is Christ Himself who is the propitiation. The remainder of the verse modifies or qualifies the term *hilasmos*. It is for our sins (*ton hamartion*, in the genitive), but not the sins of us (*ton hemeteron*) only, but those of the whole world. *Of the whole world* (*holou tou kosmou*) is genitive, thus the three terms are linked: *whole* modifies *the world*. The differences in interpretation are not due to grammar and syntax, but rather to how two key words or phrases are defined.

(5) Lexical Keys

There are two key concepts in 1 John 2:2 that help us understand the author's intended meaning, and which are disputed: propitiation (*hilasmos*), and the whole world (*holou tou kosmou*). The Greek *hilasmos* is employed in its masculine form also in 1 John 4:10, and in neuter form (*hilasterion*) in Romans 3:25 and Hebrews 9:5. The term is translated by the KJV, NASB, and the ESV as *propitiation*, which could be understood as *the place or means by which the price of sin is satisfied*. The disagreement is not on the lexical definition of the word, but on the timing of when the propitiation is applied to the individual.

Romans 3:25 identifies Jesus as publicly portrayed as a propitiation. Hebrews 9:5 refers to the mercy seat, the place where the price was paid and the forgiveness was rendered.[20] 1 John 4:10 reiterates that Jesus was sent to be a propitiation for our sins. It is important to note that the mercy seat itself did not guarantee the forgiveness of sins – the blood had to be applied properly, according to the laws pertaining to the sacrifices.

The need for proper application is foreshadowed in Exodus 12:7, 13 at the first Passover. The shedding of blood paid the price for redemption, but the application of the blood was a separate event, even if separated by only a little time. That separate event resulted in the completion of the redemption process. In the same way, Jesus could serve as a propitiation paying completely for sin, but unless His sacrifice is applied as required (through belief in Him), that price paid is not applied, and therefore sin is not forgiven. This understanding differs from the Reformed view, which does not distinguish as separate events the price paid and the application to the elect.

---

[20] The LXX translates the Hebrew *kapporeth* in Ex 25:17 as the Greek, neuter, *hilasterion*.

The second key lexical component is the phrase *the whole world* (*holou tou kosmou*). The question is whether or not *whole* is qualified or unqualified. For example, Sproul suggests – correctly, I believe – that 2 Peter 3:8-9 qualifies all (*pantes*) as all of a specific group. He observes, "The immediate antecedent of the word any in this passage is the word us, and I think it's perfectly clear that Peter is saying that God is not willing that any of us should perish, but that all of us should come to salvation. He's not speaking of all mankind indiscriminately; the us is a reference to the believing people to whom Peter is speaking."[21] Similarly, Matthew 2:2 uses the word all (*pas*), to say that all Jerusalem was troubled along with Herod. Does the all include the houses themselves in Jerusalem? The word would not require that, but seems to be making a clear reference to the *people* of Jerusalem – those who could be troubled. Likewise, Matthew 11:13 describes all (*pantes*) the prophets as prophesying until John, yet there were clearly prophets that came after John.[22] The *all* is referring to a specific group.

Thus it is not uncommon to see a contextual qualification of universal terms. But while examples of such qualification can readily be identified, it is important to recognize that qualification should only be inferred *when the context directly calls for it*. There is no textual argument – grammatical or lexical – to be made that whole does not mean whole. The only arguments offered by those holding the qualified view are theological. There is nothing in 1 John 2:2 that suggests that whole is qualified, nor any other passage that would demand that we understand the whole of 1 John 2:2 as qualified.

---

[21] Sproul, "TULIP and Reformed Theology: Limited Atonement."
[22] See Acts 21:10.

(6-7) Biblical and Theological Context

In the immediate context of 1 John 2:2, John writes to believers so that they will not sin, but if they do, he wants them to understand they have an advocate.[23] Jesus is (present tense) a propitiation for our sins – He continues to be a propitiation even today. Immediately after identifying Christ's propitiatory role, John explains the importance and reasonableness of obedience. By obedience we can have assurance of our salvation – we can know by experience (*ginosko*) that we have come to know (*ginosko*) Him. Obedience helps to provide assurance, but even when we do sin, and are thus robbed of that component of our assurance, Jesus is still our Advocate,[24] and the Holy Spirit still abides within us[25] as the pledge of our inheritance.[26] (Eph 1:13-14).

Recall John's purposes in writing: so that believers might have horizontal and vertical fellowship,[27] that his joy would be complete,[28] that believers would not sin,[29] and that they would know that they have eternal life.[30] He wants believers to understand that they are in Christ, that they should walk like it, and that their position is not conditioned on continuing obedience, but that continued obedience is necessary for their fellowship – both with God and with each other. The immediate context of 1 John 2:2 focuses on Jesus' *ongoing and present* role

---

[23] 1 John 2:1.
[24] 2:1.
[25] 3:24.
[26] Ephesians 1:13-14.
[27] 1 John 1:3.
[28] 1:4.
[29] 2:1.
[30] 5:13.

as propitiation, an idea that would seem to contradict the propitiation as being a single event.

John 11:52 is a more distant context, appealed to by MacArthur, Piper, and others, as showing that Jesus didn't die for everyone, but just for His children. Such an interpretation is dependent on the assumption that because the verse says that Jesus died for the children of God, that it means that Jesus *did not* die for those who were not the children of God. This is how MacArthur can assert that Jesus did not die for Hitler or Judas. The problem with this assumption is a logical one. The argument can be presented formally as follows:

> P1 Jesus died for the children of God.
> P2 The non-elect are not the children of God.
> C Jesus did not die for the non-elect.

This syllogism contains a conclusion that is also an assumed (unmentioned) premise. That Jesus did not die for the non-elect does not follow from a statement that He died for the children of God. Both MacArthur and Piper depend on John 11:52 to justify the *whole* of 1 John 2:2 as qualified only to the elect. But not only is the passage distant in context from John's letter, but the assertion that the passage proves Jesus did not die for the non-elect is grounded on nothing but an assumption. Further, that assumption is read back into 1 John 2:2. Finally, this interpretive justification violates the principle that the exegete must deal with the immediate context before invoking distant contexts. In both cases (the ungrounded assumption and the contextual priority problem), this is at best inadequate exegesis.

Summary of Findings

The text and translation of 1 John 2:2 give no indication that the passage is more complicated than it appears. The background and context provides no specific data that would direct us to understand the passage in a non-literal or qualified way. The textual keys and structure of the letter indicate that 2:1-2 and 2:3-6 are different pericopes, with 2:1-2 emphasizing that Christ has a *present* ministry to believers who sin, and 2:3-6 reiterating the importance of obedience for the nurturing of fellowship. The grammar and syntax indicates a straightforward, unqualified reading. Two lexical keys support the unqualified reading: the propitiation as a *present* ministry of Christ to believers, and the *whole* world as unqualified. The Biblical and theological contexts provide no textual evidence that 1 John 2:2 should be understood either entirely in the past tense or as qualified. In short, there is no exegetical evidence whatsoever to support the Reformed doctrine of limited atonement from 1 John 2:2. In this passage, at least, the indication is that God's grace is provided for all, and is accessible to all. 1 John 2:2 does not deal with how application is made, but John does address that throughout the near context, identifying belief as the means of accessing God's propitiatory grace.[31]

Conclusions and Implications

Limited atonement is a tremendously influential doctrine, in the sense that it impacts other areas of theology significantly. If we draw a limited atonement view of 1 John 2:2 when the passage was not intended to be understood that way, there are several key implications. First, we find ourselves

---

[31] 1 John 3:23, 5:1, 5:5,10, and 5:13.

misrepresenting God's character. We say He didn't die for those for whom He did. Now, on the other hand if the limited atonement view is correct, and we argue against it, then we find ourselves equally misrepresenting God's character. The entire point of John's letter is that as we are now eternally, in the present and future, children of God, we should walk like it and continue in fellowship with Him and each other. Misrepresenting God's character is no small problem for our fellowship. It is not just a theological exercise.

Second, we find ourselves misrepresenting God's work in salvation. This has serious implications for the Gospel. As Sproul indicated, limited atonement comes with other theological requirements. It is no coincidence that the Reformed position is essentially Lordship salvation, redefining repentance (as from sin, rather than a changing of the mind), and thereby redefining the Gospel. Ultimately, the question we have to answer is whether we choose what kind of God we want to believe in, or whether we instead submit to His self-revelation? Does He have the right as Sovereign Creator to tell us who He is and what He does, or are we entitled to craft Him in the image of our choosing?

17
No Time for Salvation
The *Ordo Salutis*
And the Non-necessity of Cause and Effect

Because of the Calvinistic understanding of *Total Depravity* as human inability to do anything pleasing to God, it is logically necessary that a person be temporally first regenerated in order to have faith. If faith is the one means of pleasing God, then that faith must be a gift rather than something engaged by the unsaved. On the other hand, in a competing system one is not dependent on any prevenient grace, but has the ability to believe and is simply accountable to respond in faith in order to receive regeneration, thus faith necessarily precedes regeneration.

R.C. Sproul asks important questions on the matter: "Do I cooperate with God's grace before I am born again or does the cooperation occur after? Another way of asking this question is whether to ask if regeneration is monergistic or synergistic. Is it operative or cooperative? Is it effectual or dependent?"[1] Sproul concludes on the monergistic, operative, and effectual side, asserting that faith "is not a result...of our will independently, but it is the fruit of God's sovereign act of changing the disposition of our hearts and giving to us the gift of faith."[2]

W.G.T. Shedd, coming from the Calvinistic vantage point suggests that in order to be regenerated, an unbeliever must read and hear the truth from the word, give serious application of the mind to truth, and pray for the gift of the Holy Spirit for conviction.[3] The condition of salvation, then is ultimately prayer, not faith (ever wonder where the concept of the sinners prayer came from?). Consequently, as Roy Aldrich puts it, "The extreme Calvinist deals with a rather lively spiritual corpse after all. If the corpse has enough vitality to read the Word, and heed the message, and pray for conviction, perhaps it can also believe."[4] Likewise countering the idea of regeneration preceding faith, Dan Musick concludes that because Scripture precludes completely the possibility of regeneration preceding faith, "the only reasonable conclusion is that faith precedes regeneration."[5] I would suggest there is actually a very reasonable and viable third option, and one that is more exegetically compatible with

---

[1] R.C. Sproul, "Regeneration Precedes Faith" Monergism.com, viewed at https://www.monergism.com/thethreshold/articles/onsite/sproul01.html.
[2] Nathan Bingham, "Regeneration Precedes Faith" Ligioner.org, October 9,2019, viewed at https://www.ligonier.org/blog/regeneration-precedes-faith/.
[3] W.G.T. Shedd, *Dogmatic Theology, Vol II* (New York: Windham Press, 2013), 472,512-513.
[4] Roy Aldrich, "The Gift of God" *Bibliotheca Sacra* 122:485, July 1965: 248.
[5] Dan Musick, "Faith Precedes Regeneration" Danmusicktheology.com, viewed at https://danmusicktheology.com/faith-precedes-regeneration/#34b.

the many passages showing the dependence of these two concepts on the other.

David Allen acknowledges that "it is not exegetically possible to find 'regeneration before faith' in John 1:12-13, logically or temporally."[6] As it turns out, that is the case with any passage – there are none that can be exegeted in order to rightfully infer that one precedes the other. Rather these preferences are derived from the logical relationship between cause and effect. While Allen recognizes that the principle is not exegetically driven, it is logically necessitated, and he suggests the principle in syllogistic form:

1. "Through faith" is the principle cause of "made alive."
2. Instrumental cause necessarily precedes its effect.
3. Therefore, faith precedes regeneration.[7]

Matt Slick explains how regeneration preceding faith is logically necessary: "In a light bulb, electricity must be in place for light to occur. But it is not true that light must be in place for electricity to occur. The light is dependent on the electricity, not the other way around. Therefore, electricity is logically first, but not temporally first because when the electricity is present, light is the necessary and simultaneous result."[8]

Logically, both Allen's syllogism and Slick's illustration make perfect sense. But both are deficient for demonstrating the necessity of regeneration preceding faith, or *vice versa*. Allen

---

[6] David Allen, "Does Regeneration Precede Faith?" Drdavidallen.com, April 2, 2015, viewed at http://drdavidlallen.com/baptist/does-regeneration-precede-faith/.
[7] Ibid.
[8] Matt Slick, "Does regeneration precede faith or does faith precede regeneration?" Christian Apologetics and Research Ministry, December 4, 2016, viewed at https://carm.org/does-regeneration-precede-faith.

and Slick are operating on the premise that instrumental causes necessarily precede their effects. While that is certainly true from the vantage point of temporally bound observers (which we all are), God is not bound by that limitation. Can He not engage processes concurrently that we might consider to be necessarily sequential? Certainly, He is not bound by time. In our experience He usually does seem to work within time. Still, there are obvious instances in which we are cautioned not to place our perspectives of time on Him.

Peter provides the most direct caution in 2 Peter 3:8-9, reminding his readers that God's perspectives on time are different than ours. Further, the prescience that David attributes to God is very real,[9] and yet David acknowledges that such knowledge is beyond him and unattainable.[10] Why then do we think that we must be able to work out the nuances of time that haven't been revealed in Scripture? Why do we continue to try fill in the unrevealed gaps with dogmatic philosophical assertions based on our own limited perspectives? The whole concept of cause and effect, for example, is in our own experience, and if God so chooses, He can work outside of that structure – because He created that structure. As the Sovereign Creator, He gets to define the laws of nature and the laws of logic, their scope, and their limitations.

Perhaps Calvin gets it right when, in contrast to those who call themselves Calvinists, he recognizes the tension between and interdependence of the two elements of regeneration and faith. Commenting on 1 John 5:1 he says that "no one can have faith unless he is born of God," and yet he also

---

[9] Psalm 139:15-16.
[10] Psalm 139:6.

says, "God regenerates us by faith."[11] Calvin adds that "faith is a heavenly gift...no man can believe who has not been renewed by the Spirit of God,"[12] and yet concludes transparently that, "It may be thought that the Evangelist reverses the natural order by making regeneration to precede faith, whereas, on the contrary, it is an effect of faith, and therefore ought to be placed later.[13] Calvin's own comments illustrate that there are good arguments to be made for logically preferring one event as preceding the other, and his wrestling with the tension makes it further evident that one might logically choose one over the other at the peril of ignoring the importance of the opposite perspective. In a sense, Calvin is saying that *both* regeneration and faith are logically causes *and* effects, but his conclusion speaks to temporality, as he still places these events within time.

Theologically speaking, the concept that one precedes the other *in time* is very problematic. Imagine a person begins to cross a very busy street. Just as he begins that journey, he puts his faith in Jesus, but because (in this scenario) faith precedes regeneration temporally, he has not yet been regenerated. Immediately after he believes he will be regenerated, however, in that space of time after the belief and before the moment of regeneration, this poor fellow is hit by a bus and killed instantly. (Was he hit by the bus and killed afterward, before, or concurrently? Hmmmm...) This man died a believer, but not a regenerated one. Yet that is not possible, because John 6:47 tells

---

[11] John Calvin, *Calvin's Commentaries* (1 John 5:1-5), CCEL.org, viewed at https://www.ccel.org/ccel/calvin/comment3/comm_vol45/htm/v.vi.htm.
[12] John Calvin, *Calvin's Commentaries* (John 1:6-13), CCEL.org, viewed at https://www.ccel.org/ccel/calvin/comment3/comm_vol34/htm/vii.ii.htm.
[13] Ibid.

us that the believing one has eternal life. If one is believing, he has (present tense) eternal life.

On that same busy afternoon, on the other side of the street a woman is beginning her journey across this apparently dangerous thoroughfare. As she takes her first step, because she is a Calvinist, she is regenerated. In the instant of space in between the time she is regenerated and the time she will exercise her given faith, she is struck by that very same bus, and is instantly killed. This woman died a regenerated woman, but not yet a believing one. This also is impossible, as it is the believing one who has eternal life – and the believing one will not perish, as John 3:16 clarifies.

The real lesson is perhaps not in the hypothetical and impossible spiritual journeys of these two very unfortunate people, but in their deaths by bus. While of course the death was caused by the impact of the bus, the impact and the death occurred *concurrently.* Perhaps this is one way we can come to grips with the validity of Door #3 in this case. Perhaps it is neither regeneration preceding faith, nor faith preceding regeneration, but rather both are concurrent (and maybe even interdependent) realities.

Likewise, because both are exegetically demonstrable concurrent realities, we tread on dangerous ground when we try to ascertain which is logically more important. Why not just recognize the tension of having two equally vital concepts? Perhaps it is a good reminder that when Jesus was confronted with a Door #1 or Door #2 choice, He often went through a different door altogether. In one instance, His listeners questioned Him in the synagogue, regarding whether it was lawful to heal a man on the Sabbath (Door #1) or not (Door #2). Jesus chose neither but instead explained that it was lawful to do good on the Sabbath (Door #3).[14] Later some plotted against Him and tried to trap Him by asking whether it was lawful to pay taxes to Caesar (Door #1) or not (Door #2). His response was to state an obvious principle of rendering what is due whomever it is due (Door #3).[15] His Door #3 response rendered His listeners amazed. It was simple and yet profound. Perhaps we should seek a more exegetically derived understanding rather than an understanding that provides artificial assertions derived from the logical fallacy of false dichotomy.

The arguments that regeneration must precede faith or that faith must precede regeneration are absurdities in light of what the Scriptures reveal. God as the Sovereign Creator is not bound by time, and thus is not restricted in His processes to working under those constraints. He can certainly choose to engage within time – and He does, but He is not under its governance except where He chooses to be. Because He has not answered the question in His Bible, this whole debate turns out to be much philosophical ado about nothing exegetical, yet the theological consequences are resounding and impactful.

---

[14] Matthew 12:9-12.
[15] Matthew 22:15-22.

The Sofa Rule

18
The TULIPburger

Jay Adams has a way with words, and an excellent way of explaining the significance of the doctrine of limited atonement in the Reformed view.[1] He describes the T (total depravity) and P (perseverance of the saints) as the bun, holding the burger together, and the U (unconditional election) and the I (irresistible grace) as the lettuce and tomato. But the part that makes the burger a burger is the "meat" of the L (limited atonement).

Adams suggests "To hold to the fact that Jesus didn't die for "mankind," or, as that means, persons in general—but for persons in particular, is essential to having a "Personal Savior...He didn't die for people in general, but that He knew His sheep, and called them by name, and gave His life for each one of them individually is a blessed truth, not to be omitted from the burger...Jesus didn't come to make salvation possible—He came to "seek and to save that which was lost....He didn't die needlessly for millions who would reject Him. if universal

---
[1] Jay Adams, "Tulipburger" Institute of Nouthetic Studies Blog, April 3, 2017, viewed at http://www.nouthetic.org/blog/?paged=2.

atonement were true, then God could hardly punish men and women for eternity for whom Christ had already suffered the punishment. There is no double jeopardy. And therefore, there is no burger unless it is a TULIPBURGER!"

In asserting limited atonement Adams makes four key assertions:

(1) Jesus died for people specifically, not people in general, otherwise He would not be a personal Savior.
(2) Jesus didn't just make salvation possible, he accomplished it.
(3) To die for those who would reject him would be unnecessary.
(4) To die for those who would reject Him is unjust, because it would be double jeopardy, or double punishment.

Each of these four are problematic in the light of Scripture.

Jesus didn't die for people specifically.

First, Jesus Himself speaks in general terms when describing the beneficiaries of His own death in John 3:16. Further, the "seek and save" passage narrates how Zacchaeus was saved *before* Christ died[2] – just like Abraham before him.[3] As Ephesians 2:8-9 describes, grace is the means through the vehicle of faith whereby the gift of salvation is applied to the believer. Even Caiaphas recognized that Jesus would die for "the people."[4] In John 8:24 Jesus proclaims in the temple a warning to all who were present that they needed to believe in order to avoid dying in their sins. While many believed,[5] not all did. Jesus made the offer to all – even to those who would not believe. Why would He *not* have provided, in addition to His offer, a way

---

[2] Luke 19:10.
[3] Genesis 15:6.
[4] John 11:50.
[5] John 8:30.

for them to receive what He had offered? Here is a case of false dichotomy: we are not left with only two choices (that Jesus died for people in general, or that He died for people specifically). The answer is simply all of the above. Jesus died for all generally, and every individual specifically.

Jesus didn't just make salvation possible, He accomplished it.

If He accomplished salvation on the cross, then where is the need for faith? The doctrine of regeneration preceding faith takes care of that. According to this particular brand of Calvinism, God has regenerated the person before they had faith, in order that they would have faith. But consider God's own metaphor of the salvific process: the Passover. Exodus 12:7, and 12:12-13 describe how the Israelites had to *apply* the blood of the lamb in order to be saved.

An Israelite could kill the lamb, but if the blood wasn't applied to the doorposts, the angel of death would not spare the firstborn of that household. Again, Door #3 is the correct answer here: it appears that neither regeneration precedes faith nor faith precedes regeneration, but that they are concurrent. Also, Peter recounts how Gentiles were told they would be given words *by which they would be saved* (Acts 11:14) – the verb is future active indicative. It had not yet been accomplished when the message was given. Christ's death didn't save them, their appropriate response to Him was the vehicle that completed the transaction.

To die for those who would reject him would be unnecessary.

This statement assumes that the only purpose for His death was to accomplish salvation. However, His death demonstrated also His worthiness to receive glory,[6] it served as an opportunity for Him to be submissive to the Father, and ultimately receive glory.[7] While His death was necessary for more than just the salvation of those who would receive it, whether necessary or necessary is not the issue. Whether or not Jesus died for all is. John explains that Jesus is the propitiation (satisfaction, *hilasmos*) for the sins not only of "us," but also of the whole world.[8]

To die for those who would reject Him is unjust, because it would be double jeopardy, or double punishment.

In Christ, the Father was reconciling the world to Himself,[9] and Paul is entreating people to be reconciled to God.[10] Christ died once to pay for sins – just for unjust,[11] just as one act of Adam brought condemnation for all men, the death of Christ brought "justification of life" to all men.[12] Jesus died once, was forsaken by His Father once,[13] and in doing that He covered all sin for all humanity. It was one sacrifice for all, once and for all.

Does that mean that all are saved? No. Notice the distinction between "all" in Romans 5:18, and "many" in 5:19. To all were brought justification of life through Christ's death, but the result is that many will be made righteous, not all. Those that are not made righteous still had their sins paid for (just like any Israelite who had slain the lamb at Passover), but they

---

[6] Revelation 5:12.
[7] Philippians 2:5-9.
[8] 1 John 2:2.
[9] 2 Corinthians 5:19.
[10] 5:20.
[11] Hebrews 7:27, 1 Peter 3:18.
[12] Romans 5:18.
[13] Matthew 27:46.

simply have not applied the death of Christ to their own account (just like any Israelite who had not put the blood on the doorposts).

The wages of sin is death. That is an eternal penalty, and can never be paid off by the individual who is attempting to pay it. In Christ's death, He brought to humanity a way for their account to be resolved. As we see in Abraham's case, the belief in the Lord was accounted to him as righteousness,[14] but Abraham's sin still had to be covered. Christ's death later was the payment for sin that God required in order to remain just in crediting righteousness to Abraham. Paul refers to the gospel as the ability (or power) of God to save people.[15] All are condemned and under sin,[16] but all who believe in Jesus Christ are justified as a gift by His grace.[17] This gospel of personal salvation is to be preached to all creation.[18] Some will believe, some will not. Jesus has already paid for the sins of all. For those who don't believe, their sin is paid for, but not applied to their account. That is the simple lesson of the Passover event. Salvation is by grace *through faith.*

To say that God can't use double jeopardy sounds catchy, but it places God under a western judicial principle that He simply isn't obligated by. Further, there are no "overages" in payment for sin (hence, no double jeopardy or double punishment). The application of grace is and has always been through the vehicle of faith in Him. To suggest that salvation is

---

[14] Genesis 15:6.
[15] Romans 1:16-17.
[16] 3:9.
[17] 3:22-24.
[18] Mark 16:15-16.

accomplished apart from faith is contrary to that longstanding principle that the just shall live by faith.[19]

With all due love and respect to Jay Adams and others who hold to TULIP, this is one of the rare occasions when I will skip the burger and enjoy another meal instead. Exegetically, the TULIPburger isn't quite right – just too many artificial ingredients.

---

[19] Habakkuk 2:4.

19
The History of the Problem of Evil

The seemingly unavoidable contradiction between the existence of a personal God and the reality of evil provides a crucial point of entry not only for discussion both of (1) argument for and against the existence of God and (2) the nature and character of such a God, but also, as Neiman suggests, the problem of evil is itself an organizing principle for history of philosophy.[1] Thus the theologian will not be the only interlocutor on the subject, but rather in fact the philosopher must also dedicate significant energies to understanding and ultimately dealing with the problem. Perhaps if Neiman is correct, the problem has even less to do with philosophy of religion than with philosophy itself, or then again, as I would suggest the problem of evil affords *an example of the unbreakable bond between religion and philosophy and the resultant necessity of interdisciplinarity between the two.*

Noting the significance, then, of the issue, this present discussion will (1) identify major theorists and their statements

---
[1] Susan Neiman, *Evil in Modern Thought* (Princeton, NJ: Princeton University Press, 2002), 7.

of the problem within context, and (2) will give attention to various attempts at resolution also within a chronological context. I will neither offer critiques of these various attempts nor propose a theodicy, nor will I attempt to offer a comprehensive discussion of pertinent thinkers and their views. The focus here will be an introductory survey intended to provide a working and historically informed definition of the problem of evil from theological and philosophical vantage points.

Introduction

Just as philosophical inquiry has a grand tradition of attempting paradox resolution, it is often these very same postulated resolutions that create further paradoxes. In Presocratic natural philosophy, for example, Parmenides, seeking to ground monism more appropriately proposed a theory of reality which suggested that reality was both motionless and limited, thus requiring his 'cue-ball' kind of world – spherical and homogeneous.[2] His cosmology begs questions though – questions such as how motion can be accounted for in a motionless reality and how pluralities which can be observed in appearance can be accounted for in a singular reality.

While Parmenides certainly attempts to resolve these issues, the questions give rise to further evolution in thought – note the shift from monism to pluralism. Empedocles proposes an entire cosmology which would justify Parmenides' approach but which would also deal with the paradox of appearances more effectively. To accomplish this feat, Empedocles develops a

---

[2] W.K.C. Guthrie, *A History of Greek Philosophy Vol. II: The Presocratic tradition from Parmenides to Democritus* (Cambridge: Cambridge University Press, 1965), 34-46.

position that includes four elements (air, water, earth, and fire) and two significant forces (love and strife). With each advance and development, the cosmologies grow more and more complex and the questions grow more difficult.

This kind of dilemma is not unique to Presocratic natural philosophy, but also finds its way into later metaphysics. The problem of evil (both moral and natural) is one such issue which, when historically examined, exemplifies the predicament of creating more questions than answers. Can it be said that the problem of evil is a mere creation of philosophical inquiry, or is it a case study for paradox resolution within philosophical inquiry? How is Neiman (for example) justified in identifying evil (and its related problems) as the underlying issue in history of philosophy? An examination of the problem as defined and dealt with in historical context can go a long way in helping us to come to grips with the significance and structure of the problem itself, and can perhaps provide an impetus for resolution.

The Problem of Evil in Ancient Philosophy

Preliminary Religious Characterizations

Most conservative biblical scholars acknowledge the book of Job as one of the earliest biblical books, dating its content around 2000 BC, and contemporary to patriarchal times (i.e., Abraham, etc.). As such, Job provides a very early inquiry into the purpose of evil. Job 10:7 offers Job's essential statement of the problem: "According to Thy knowledge I am indeed not guilty; yet there is no deliverance from Thy hand." Job here questions God's allowance of evil in his life despite his perceived innocence. Eliphaz, Bildad, and Zophar all rebuke Job, presenting as a theodicy the idea that God possesses a kind of justice which would only allow evil for punishment of sin, and concludes that Job must have been stained by sin.

Yet another perspective arises, that of Elihu, who argues that Surely, God will not act wickedly, and the Almighty will not pervert justice...If He should determine to do so, if He should gather to Himself His spirit and His breath, all flesh would perish together and man would return to dust."(34:12,14-15) Elihu's argument revolves around the character of God being unimpeachable and unquestionable. The problem of evil in the book of Job is not that evil exists, but rather that the presence of evil at times does not seem justified by circumstances. This perspective on the problem is represented regularly in later biblical texts such as Habakkuk[3] (7th century BC), and Romans[4] (1st century AD). Throughout the biblical record there is arguable univocality in favor of a theodicy.

Zoroastrianism is decidedly dualistic and monotheistic. In one particular strain Ahura Mazda (Ormuzd) is the benevolent deity in opposition to the evil Ahriman who possessed nearly equal power. Ormuzd, lacking the ability at present to fully eradicate evil, cannot be described as fully omnipotent, but will one day possess such capability, at which point evil will be eliminated. Thus history is outlined by the struggle against evil – a struggle which will at some point have a resolution which will in itself eliminate not only evil, but

---

[3] Habakkuk questions God directly as to how He can tolerate sinfulness (the presence of evil) without bringing about immediate judgment, and then later how God can use the wicked as instruments of judgment against those who are seemingly far less wicked.

[4] Particularly in chapter 9, perhaps anticipating and offering resolution to Epicurus' riddle.

consequently any paradoxes associated with the existence of evil.

The Qur'an presents Allah as responsible for both good and evil, doing what he wishes (Qur'an 3:40) even to the point of testing by instrument of both good and evil (Qur'an 21:35), and thus the Qur'an does not concern itself with resolution. In fact, there has been little systematic emphasis on theodicy within Islam. Later traditions do point to the need for evil as a kind of resistive complement to the moral.[5]

While the Judeo-Christian, Zoroastrian, and Islamic bases are more univocal in their responses – owing to a primarily monotheistic starting point – polytheistic, pantheistic, and non-theistic traditions place lesser emphasis on the need for resolution to the problem of evil, as they essentially do not hold to the existence of the kind of deity whose existence alongside that of evil that would create a significant paradox. Yet they all must deal with the existence and origin of suffering and evil in at least some regard, and most of them do in various degree.

Hindu tradition provides diversity in addressing the issue. At least three particular varieties of description can be identified: (1) that of the Vedas, which present an ongoing dualistic (good vs. evil) conflagration, (2) that of the pantheistic literature (Upanishads, etc.), which relates evil to the cosmic cycle in relation to karma, and (3) that of the Epics and Puranas, which describe a kind of anthropomorphic theism in which the gods are responsible for both good and evil. Rem Edwards suggests that Eastern religions (including both Hinduism and Buddhism) "fully develop the idea that evil originates in sheer finitude and fragmentariness of perspective and in the desire for

---

[5] Mian Mohammed Sharif, *A History of Muslim Philosophy* (Wiesbaden: Harrassowitz, 1966), 1658.

fragmentary goals and objects…and see evil as originating to some extent in immorality, for the sufferings of this world are partly if not entirely the working out of one's Karma."[6]

While not tendering a systematic theodicy – particular in the matter of the origin of evil – Hinduism does offer a means of dealing with the existence of evil and (at least) minimizing its effect: namely, the eternality of the soul provides a setting (through a sequence of births and temporal existence) whereby one can learn to avoid ignorance and associated actions which afford negative karmic results – including suffering and evil.

Not unlike Hindu explanations, the Buddhist approach to evil and suffering is largely characterized by the relationship of evil to karma.

Buddhism posits the *Four Noble Truths,*[7] in which suffering can be limited and even eliminated by the right kinds of thought and action. However, a key distinguishing characteristic of Buddhism is its rejection of the existence of an omnibenevolent (or any other) deity, with partial justification in the asserted paradox of evil, as presented in the following verses from the 13th century *Bhuridatta Jataka:*

> If the creator of the world entire
> They call God, of every being be the Lord
> Why does he order such misfortune
> And not create concord?
> If the creator of the world entire
> They call God, of every being be the Lord

---

[6] Rem B. Edwards, *Reason and Religion: An Introduction to the Philosophy of Religion* (New York: Harcourt Brace Jovanovich, Inc., 1972), 28.
[7] (1) the existence of impermanence, (2) the cause of suffering is craving (3) cessation of suffering comes by cessation of craving, and (4) the means is the middle way, or eightfold path.

> Why prevail deceit, lies and ignorance
> And he such inequity and injustice create?
> If the creator of the world entire
> They call God, of every being be the Lord
> Then an evil master is he, (O Aritta)
> Knowing what's right did let wrong prevail![8]

Bearing marked resemblance to Epicurus' riddle, these verses illustrate an aspect of the grounding for Buddhist rejection of theism. There is, within Buddhist tradition, no need for a theologically driven theodicy, yet the paradox of suffering still exists without explanation.

Within the various religious traditions there is broad agreement that evil exists and that it is a central theme in the comparative doctrines, yet justification for the existence of evil and magnitude of the paradox differs significantly from belief system to belief system. While each system gives at least some attention to the problem, it seems readily apparent that within the Christian tradition one will find the greatest consideration of and more numerous propositions for resolution of the problem. Perhaps the problem of evil is a central issue for the biblical system, since it is more *precisely* definitive of the character of God than it is in any other system.

Plato (428-348)

In Plato's dialogue between Socrates and Euthyphro, Socrates asks "Is the pious loved by the gods because it is pious, or is it pious because it is loved by the gods?" The question reflects a dilemma related to the problem of evil. If the former is

---

[8] As translated by V.A. Gunasekara, in *The Buddhist Attitude to God*, viewed at
http://www.buddhistinformation.com/buddhist_attitude_to_god.htm.

affirmed, then the gods are governed by an absolute standard which would necessarily be superior to them by virtue of its governance. If the latter is affirmed, then any absolute standard of piety (or goodness) must be dismissed. If the latter is affirmed then the gods (or God) could not accurately be described as absolutely good since there would be no absolute standard of good, but again if the former is affirmed then the gods (or God) could not be described as all powerful, since they (or He) would be governed by piety (or goodness).

While Plato provides an epistemological basis for further discussion of the problem of evil, he would not have recognized the existence of evil as presenting any difficulty to explain. Evil offers a counterbalance to good and "evils can never pass away, for there must always remain something which is antagonistic to good."[9] Regarding moral evil (absence of good, virtue, etc., related to ignorance), it is to the soul as physical evil (disease) is to the body – each type of evil brings about the destruction of its host.[10] In life and death comes a kind of divine justice, as Plato's *Apology* recounts Socrates statement that "no evil can happen to a good man either in life or after death."[11] But the very existence of evil is attributed in the *Timaeus* to the demiurge's creation not as *ex nehilo*, but rather from preexisting and imperfect materials. Here Plato identifies a dichotomy in causation between the necessary and the divine, the latter of which is recognizable as nature permits happiness, and the former being prerequisite to the divine.[12] While Plato did believe in the benevolence of the deity, he would not accept the premise

---

[9] Plato, *Theaetetus*, 176.
[10] Plato, *Republic*, Book X, 608.
[11] Plato, *Apology*, 41d.
[12] Plato, Timaeus, 36:69.

of the creative deity possessing omnipotence, thus in Platonic thinking there is no paradox regarding the existence of evil, for it is necessary.

Epicurus (341-270)

Although there is no extant form of Epicurus' characterization of the problem, he is generally credited as the first to state it, and he does so in the form of a trilemma, which as understood by Hume could be structured as follows: if God is omnipotent, omniscient, and omnibenevolent, then how can evil exist in a world made by God? First century (BC) atomist Lucretius represents significant Epicurean influence, and his poem *De Rerum Natura* provides an important source for Epicurean doctrine, as Lucretius argues against the teleological on grounds (among others) that there is frailty and evil present for which cannot be accounted in a teleological system. Third century theologian Lanctantius provides perhaps the strongest early evidence of Epicurus' statement of the trilemma, as he propounds an apologetic responding directly to Epicurus:

> What happiness, then, can there be in God, if He is always inactive, being at rest and un-moveable? if He is deaf to those who pray to Him, and blind to His worshippers? [lacking omniscience] What is so worthy of God, and so befitting to Him, as providence? [lacking omnipotence] But if He cares for nothing [lacking omnibenevolence], and foresees nothing, He has lost all His divinity [note: Epicurus' necessary conclusion]. What else does he say, who takes from God all power and all substance, except that there is no God at all? [notes mine].[13]

And again, regarding two particular horns of the problem:

---

[13] Lactantius, *On the Anger of God.*

> God, says Epicurus, regards nothing [premise 1: lacking omnibenevolence]; therefore He has no power [conclusion: lacking omnipotence]. For he who has power must of necessity regard affairs [premise 2: inferential relationship between omnibenevolence and omnipotence]. For if He has power, and does not use it, what so great cause is there that, I will not say our race, but even the universe itself, should be contemptible in His sight?[14]

While Epicurus' goal was not to assert atheism (he didn't, but rather posited that if gods existed they were of no concern, being themselves either unconcerned or impotent regarding human affairs), his elucidation of the problem of evil in particular and resultant complexities in the teleological idea provides momentum for the atheistic worldview, and thus with Epicurus (as characterized by Lucretius, Lactantius, and later Hume) the problem of evil becomes a pivot point of discussion not only in regard to theism but cosmogony and cosmology in general. The teleological nature of the issue causes the problem of evil to be of significance to a number of fields within philosophical inquiry.

Plotinus (205-270)

Relating evil to matter itself, Plotinus sees matter as having potential for good but being in itself (and unaided) a primary evil. While this in itself seems a significant contradiction in Plotinus' approach, his characterization of evil not as an objective state of being but rather as the absence (although not completely so) of good importantly provides the Neoplatonic context for iteration and solution of the problem. Evil is in the realm of non-being. Plotinus explains:

> If such be the Nature of Beings and of That which transcends all the realm of Being, Evil cannot have place among Beings or in the

---

[14] Ibid.

> Beyond- Being; these are good. *There remains, only, if Evil exist at all, that it be situate in the realm of Non- Being,* [emphasis mine] that it be some mode, as it were, of the Non- Being, that it have its seat in something in touch with Non- Being or to a certain degree communicate in Non- Being. By this Non- Being, of course, we are not to understand something that simply does not exist, but only something of an utterly different order from Authentic-Being: there is no question here of movement or position with regard to Being; the Non- Being we are thinking of is, rather, an image of Being or perhaps something still further removed than even an image. Now this (the required faint image of Being) might be the sensible universe with all the impressions it engenders, or it might be something of even later derivation, accidental to the realm of sense, or again, it might be the source of the sense-world or something of the same order entering into it to complete it. Some conception of it would be reached by thinking of measurelessness as opposed to measure, of the unbounded against bound, the unshaped against a principle of shape, the ever-needy against the self-sufficing: think of the ever-undefined, the never at rest, the all -accepting but never sated, utter dearth; and make all this character not mere accident in it but its equivalent for essential- being, so that, whatsoever fragment of it be taken, that part is all lawless void, while whatever participates in it and resembles it becomes evil, though not of course to the point of being, as itself is, Evil-Absolute.[15]

Plotinus' dichotomy is evident: being and beyond-being is good, and while non-being does indeed exist, it is essentially distinct from authentic being. Thus evil does not exist as an objective hypostasis, and certainly not as a co-equal and opposing force to deity.

The impact that the Neoplatonic definition of evil would have on future discussion is truly immeasurable, and Plotinus' characterization is an instinctive entry point for the medieval philosophers.

---

[15] Plotinus, *Enneads*, 8:3.

The Problem of Evil in Medieval Philosophy
It is early in this era that we see a turn toward more theological interpretations of the problem, and perhaps for two reasons: (1) As the rise in philosophy observed in the presocratics can be attributed to directed effort toward naturalistic explanations, there was a reluctance on the part of more than a few to adopt the materialist framework. While natural philosophy was constructing the problem and attempting materialist solutions, moral philosophy was not immune to the pursuit and found itself in need of similarly contrived resolutions on the topic. Also of significance, (2) natural philosophy declined (at least) with Socrates' shift toward moral philosophy and perhaps can be credited to lack of development in contemporary scientific methods. The naturalists could only extend tested theories so far, thus microcosm presented greater need and opportunity for advancement than did macrocosm. But how to explain the human experience relating to interaction with evil in metaphysical terms? This question would find primacy in the philosophy of the medievals.

Gnosticism
As a developed synthesis of Platonic cosmogony (as presented in *Timaeus*) and epistemological premises gnosticism found itself impacting the problem. Evil's existence, in gnostic tradition, was attributed to the failure of the demiurge's potency – an absolute denial of omnipotence, and thus as in Plato, the problem of evil was a non-issue. Such justifications on grounds of rejecting omnipotence were untenable to the groundings of the Western theological minds that would soon rise as the Biblical

text became a focal point for the bonding of theological presupposition with philosophical justification.

In practice the foundations of gnosticism were characteristically dualistic, viewing the material as corrupt and that relating to gnosis as purer. As a result, two particular strains of orthodoxy become evident: (1) that which would de-emphasize the significance of the material/corrupt and thus promote licentiousness, and (2) that which would highlight the significance of the material/corrupt and in accordance promote asceticism. Later thinkers would respond (generally) critically toward both.

Irenaeus (c115-c200)

Working from a theistic standpoint and a Biblical context, Irenaeus opposed Gnostic premises, responding directly to them (perhaps most notably in *Against Heresies*). He affirmed omnipotence and offered an alternative solution in two forms. First, Irenaeus redefined the epistemological grounding on the issue, appealing to the Biblical text as the source of objective truth, consequently dismissing Platonic cosmogony as untenable.

Second, he redefined anthropological cosmogony, operating from the basic premise that human free will is prerequisite to human good or perfection. This presupposes that God did not create perfection (in mankind at least). Rather perfection comes through the proper appropriation of autonomy. While natural evil provides opportunity and occasion for the person's growth, moral evil is then an outcome of free will appropriated to disobedience, and is not due directly or necessarily to the corporeal nature of humanity (as in gnosticism). He is specific on this point, saying,

> Those persons, then, who possess the earnest of the Spirit, and who are not enslaved by the lusts of the flesh, but are subject to the Spirit, and who in all things walk according to the light of reason, does the apostle properly term "spiritual," because the Spirit of God dwells in them. *Now, spiritual men shall not be incorporeal spirits; but our substance, that is, the union of flesh and spirit, receiving the Spirit of God, makes up the spiritual man* [emphasis mine].[16]

Thus the spiritual man is one who has received the Spirit of God in union with the flesh (and spirit). In gnostic tradition such redemption of the flesh would have been impossible, yet for Irenaeus, in accordance with his epistemological foundationalism (holding revelation as foundational) is able to argue for a theodicy that neither denies the omnipotence of God nor the existence of evil. While he would certainly face significant hermeneutic challenges in defending his conception of man and his place in the cosmos, he nevertheless succeeds in providing an alternative in both areas of knowledge and cosmogony of evil, and as a result is influential in restructuring the debate. Also notable here is the role given to free will, which further colors future discussion and again illustrates the centrality of the problem of evil in connecting philosophy and theology.

Augustine (354-430)

From his foundational assertion that God is "supremely and equally and unchangeably good,"[17] Augustine argues admittedly[18] from the Neoplatonic standpoint that evil is the

---

[16] Irenaeus, *Against Heresies*, 5: 8:2.
[17] Augustine, *Enchiridion*, 10-12.
[18] Augustine, *Confessions*, 7:9:13.

The History of the Problem of Evil   165

privation of good. He distinguishes between natural evil as penal consequence and moral evil as the fruit of free will appropriated in disobedience. Augustine attributes significance to the existence of evil, but not at the expense of God's omnipotence or omnibenevolence. Thus evil must serve those two qualities in a utilitarian sense. He says,

> And in the universe, even that which is called evil, when it is regulated and put in its own place, only enhances our admiration of the good; for we enjoy and value the good more when we compare it with the evil. For the almighty God, who, as even the heathen acknowledge, has supreme power over all things, being Himself supremely good, would never permit the existence of anything evil among His works, if He were not so omnipotent and good that He can bring good even out of evil. For what is that which we call evil but the absence of good?[19]

Evil is only allowed inasmuch as God is powerful enough to bring from it greater good. And Augustine is careful to characterize evil not as not as an independent substance of equal quality to that of the good, but rather simply as the absence of good. In illustration of this he discusses a wound as a defect in the flesh which when health is restored ceases to exist. The wound does not continue existence elsewhere, and thus should not be seen as an entity in itself but rather as the privation of function or health. Evil functions in the same manner.

It should also be noted that Augustine believed good to be extracted from evil even to the point of *supreme* good. Evil contributes in an important way to cosmic order: privation of good is a necessary and divine implement serving an almost aesthetic overview of existence. The principle of plenitude begins to emerge here. Finally, for Augustine, evil finds its origin and

---

[19] Augustine, *Enchiridion*, 10-12.

impetus as being intimately connected to human free will. God in His goodness allows free will, the utilization of which must possibly result in a turning from God. Augustine notes that the turning itself is the central issue, not the alternative chosen. He says,

> For when the will relinquishes that which is superior to itself, and turns to that which is inferior, it becomes evil not because that toward which it turns is evil, but because the turning is evil.[20]

Thus the turning itself results in the privation of the ideal and offers contingencies not readily identifiable with any overall good, yet when viewed in perspective of the whole, there is an aesthetic sense in which the whole is (and must be) deemed good. This creates another problem separate yet related problem with which Augustine must deal – and one beyond the scope of this present discussion: the compatibility of human free will with the divine perfections of omniscience, omnipotence, and omnibenevolence. The manner in which he deals with these issues necessarily impacts his conception of theodicy.

Anselm of Canterbury (1033-1109)

Anselm, like Augustine, preferred to see creature-volition as the means whereby the responsibility for the existence of evil is placed elsewhere other than at the feet of God, and in so doing protected the attribute of omnibenevolence, a necessary consequence to his ontological defense of the existence of God. Anselm's argument is as follows:

> something greater than which cannot be thought exists in thought...And certainly that greater than which cannot be

---

[20] Augustine, *City of God*, 12:3.

> understood cannot exist only in thought, for if it exists only in thought it could also be thought of as existing in reality as well, which is greater. If, therefore, that than which greater cannot be thought exists in thought alone, then that than which greater cannot be thought turns out to be that than which something greater actually can be thought, but that is obviously impossible. Therefore something than which greater cannot be thought undoubtedly exists both in thought and in reality.²¹

The argument requires 'that than which greater cannot be thought' to possess the highest degree of perfection, and thus Anselm narrows the debate to exclude the possibility of diminishing the perfections of God in order to resolve the problem of evil. For Anselm, as was also the case with Augustine, creature-volition seemed the best option. In discussing freedom of the will, Anselm emphasizes not freedom *from* but rather freedom *to*. This active element of freedom does not, for Anselm, in its protection especially of omnibenevolence, violate omnipotence or omniscience, despite its potential to create scenarios which could be described as evil, as that freedom finds its very origin and enablement in divine mandate. The significant contribution here is the centrality of omnibenevolence in the trilemma.

Aquinas (1225-1274)

Isaiah 45:7 reads in the KJV as follows: "I form the light, and create darkness: I make peace, and create evil: I the Lord do all these things." Aquinas counters a syllogistic argument based on this passage:

(P1) God created everything,
(P2) Evil is something,

---

²¹ Anselm, *Proslogion*, David Barr, (trans.), Ch. 2.

(C) Therefore, God created evil.

The second premise causes difficulty for Aquinas as he, consistent with Neoplatonic thinking, argues against evil as a *substance*. He says,

> . . . As the term good signifies 'perfect being', so the term evil signifies nothing else than 'privation of perfect being'. In its proper acceptance, privation is predicated of that which is fitted by its nature to be possessed, and to be possessed at a certain time and in a certain manner. Evidently, therefore, a thing is called evil if it lacks a perfection it ought to have. Thus if a man lacks the sense of sight, this is an evil for him. But the same lack is not an evil for a stone, for the stone is not equipped by nature to have the faculty of sight.[22]

Aquinas solidifies for medieval philosophy the definition of evil as privation rather than essence. Like those before him he recognizes that this definition requires human volition in order to account for privation, and that evil as a penalty is introduced by God in order to supply justice. This accommodation is a significant one, as it additionally introduces an intersection between theological philosophy and naturalistic philosophy by way of a world ordered by justice. The teleological emphasis here ties the problem of evil and theodicies of this order to the concepts of necessity, justice, and plenitude – factors not exclusive to the religious or the secular, but rather shared by both. Thus while Aquinas remains perhaps the medieval era's most provocative advocate of theological philosophy, he also plays an important role in uniting the interests of the religious

---

[22] From Thomas Aquinas, *Compendium theologiae* 114, 125-126, as quoted in Bill King, "Thomas Aquinas on the Metaphysical Problem of Evil" in *Quodlibet Journal*, Vol. 4, No. 2-3, Summer 2002.

and the secular as he frames the problem of evil in terms which can be engaged from either grounding.

William of Ockham (1288-1347)

Whereas previous thinkers regarded omnibenevolence as the attribute least predisposed to redefinition, Ockham shared no such regard. He suggested that there existed in the volition of God distinction between *potentia absoluta* (absolute power) and *potentia ordinata* (ordained power). Feinberg explains the division:

> The distinction between the two powers doesn't mean that God acts sometimes with order and other times without it. It means that God can, and has, in fact, decided to do certain things according to the laws which He *freely* establishes, i.e., de potentia ordinata. On the other hand, God has absolute power (potentia absoluta) to do anything that doesn't imply a contradiction...[23]

The result for Ockham is a non-absolute standard of good: God is not obligated to act in a certain manner because that action is good, rather it is good because He declares it to be so. Thus in Ockham's estimation the standard of good is God Himself. Some, like Barnhart, believe that such a move robs the term *goodness* of any real meaning and results in a cruel and tyrannical deity. Barnhart indicts such a deity as

> ...not only [knowing] who would go to hell, he actually created them to go there...[this] is not unfair because God is not subject to the principle of fairness. He is above it.[24]

---

[23] John S. Feinberg, *The Many Faces of Evil: Theological Systems and the Problems of Evil* (Wheaton, IL: Crossway, 2004), 37.
[24] Joe E. Barnhart, *The Billy Graham Religion* (Philadelphia, PA: Pilgrim Press, 1972), 135.

For Ockham, this redefinition represented an ironclad theodicy, but it invited criticism as the very nature of good and God was in need of reassessment. Such analysis would be furthered with the dawn of the Reformation and the rise of the Modern Era of philosophy.

The Problem of Evil in Modern Philosophy

Calvin (1509-1564)

Calvin resolutely disregards human volition as a means of absolving God for evil's existence, and thus rejects earlier mainstream theodicies. In Ockham, however, Calvin finds an agreeable response to the problem, and builds upon Ockham's foundation – his conception of good. Calvin minces no words when describing the root of good:

> The will of God is the supreme rule of righteousness, so that everything which he wills must be held to be righteous by the mere fact of his willing it. Therefore, when it is asked why the Lord did so, we must answer, Because he pleased. But if you proceed farther to ask why he pleased, you ask for something greater and more sublime than the will of God, and nothing such can be found.[25]

Calvin's lofty view of God excels his concept of good as a standard. God is Himself the standard, and as in Ockham, the problem of evil, at least as formally conceived disintegrates. A new problem, however, rises in its place – the nature of divine justice. Calvin anticipates this, offering,

---

[25] John Calvin, *Institutes of the Christian Religion*, Henry Beveridge, trans., 3:23:2.

First, they ask why God is offended with his creatures who have not provoked him by any previous offense; for to devote to destruction whomsoever he pleases, more resembles the caprice of a tyrant than the legal sentence of a judge; and, therefore, there is reason to expostulate with God, if at his mere pleasure men are, without any desert of their own, predestinated to eternal death. If at any time thoughts of this kind come into the minds of the pious, they will be sufficiently armed to repress them, by considering how sinful it is to insist on knowing the causes of the divine will, since it is itself, and justly ought to be, the cause of all that exists. For if his will has any cause, there must be something antecedent to it, and to which it is annexed; this it were impious to imagine.

For Calvin, not only is God the standard of good, but also that of order. He supplies a teleological grounding based in His volition and acting as causative of all things. All things, then, work in accordance with His justice, and that justice imbues the cosmos with order much like paint encompasses the canvas and provides the implement for intelligibility of meaning and design in the resulting artwork.

Descartes (1596-1560)

Descartes follows Augustinian theory in two particular areas: (1) assertion of human volition, and (2) evil as a non-essence. But Descartes adds an important component to the discussion. To this point omnipotence was the attribute most commonly limited in efforts to construct a theodicy. Descartes focuses on this feature as well, but rather than limiting it he expands it to the degree that God can even perform contradictions if He so desires. This is related to the idea of contingency that Descartes supports, as Nussbaum explains,

> For him, not only is it the case that causal laws could have been different, had God willed it so; more radically, the laws of mathematics and of logic themselves could have been different as well.[26]

Thus God could have chosen other permutations of organizing laws, but in accord with Anselm's view of the perfection of God, Descartes recognizes that this world is the best possible, and that as God determines what laws will be, they then become necessary. Contingency, then, exists but with limits at the point where the contingent becomes the real. At this point the real becomes necessary. So while Descartes does utilize the free-will explanation in his theodicy, two additional ingredients are observable: (1) the possibility of contradiction due to superomnipotence, or the divine possession of power which can contradict without self-defeat, generates a course in which the problem of evil becomes a non sequitur, and (2) his concept of contingency which offers a teleological explanation for the presence of evil. It should be noted in this context that in addition to these specific theodical elements, Descartes also provides an intersection of philosophy and theology, as his theodicy is distinctly philosophical. Janowski observes that

> *Descartes' prime concern is Certitude or Truth* [emphasis mine], while the classical theodicies deal with the existence of moral evil...Although Descartes tried not to meddle with theological and moral issues, it is clear from his treatment of the good and the true – both of which, according to him, were established by God – that they are two aspects of the same problem.[27]

---

[26] Charles Nussbaum, "Aesthetics and the Problem of Evil," in *Metaphilosophy*, Vol. 34, No. 3, April 2003.
[27] Zbigniew Janowski, *Cartesian Theodicy: Descartes' Quest for Certitude* (Norwell, MA: Kluwer Academic Publishers, 2000), 13.

The History of the Problem of Evil   173

For Descartes epistemological consistency, grounded in reason, was central in his theodicy, thus expanding discussions of theodicy into the realm of epistemology.

Spinoza (1632-1677)

Spinoza adopts, as Nussbaum categorizes him, a primarily modal approach to theodicy, espousing causal determinism and advocating necessity rather than contingency. Whereas Spinoza acknowledges contingency in an epistemological sense, he categorically denies it in the natural sense.[28] Spinoza's affinity for necessity corresponds with his emphasis on plenitude (Lovejoy's term) – the idea that all that can be must be. With a view toward a 'greater good' theodicy, Spinoza held that all that exists must do so of necessity. Evil exists in similar fashion to the Neoplatonic conception as privation rather than essence – on this point Spinoza agrees with Augustine. The point of departure for Spinoza is causation, whereas Augustine viewed evil as caused by wrongheaded choices, Spinoza perceives evil as that which is suffered due to external forces acting on the individual. Yet good and evil are not absolute, as he describes in *The Ethics*, they both emerge equally from the perfect nature of a (panentheistic) deity:

> If all things follow from a necessity of the absolutely perfect nature of God, why are there so many imperfections in nature? Such, for instance, as things corrupt to the point of putridity, loathsome deformity, confusion, evil, sin, etc....the perfection of things is to be reckoned only from their own nature and power; things are not more or less perfect, according as they delight or offend the human senses, or according as they are serviceable or repugnant to mankind.[29]

---

[28] Nussbaum, Ibid.
[29] Spinoza, *The Ethics*, Part I, Appendix.

The elements of necessity and perfection are in view for Spinoza, and flowing from his panentheistic perspective of God – He does not make creative determinations but rather supports and sustains by way of omnipotence – Spinoza creates for himself tremendous latitude in defining of good. The principle of perfection when conjoined with necessity yields varying degrees of perfection including evil as privation of higher degrees of the same. He says in this regard,

> To those who ask why God did not so create all men, that they should be governed only by reason, I give no answer but this: because matter was not lacking to him for the creation of every degree of perfection from highest to lowest; or more strictly, because the laws of his nature are so vast, as to suffice for the production of everything conceivable by an infinite intelligence...[30]

Here is a form of greater-good theodicy which must of necessity include each degree of perfection, even to the negative extreme. Spinoza's theodicy, due to its emphasis on plenitude, invites aesthetic critique rather than purely rational assessment, thus affording a point of intersection between philosophical critique and theological dogma.

Leibniz (1646-1716)

For Leibniz, the problem of evil is a supreme inquiry. He seems particularly motivated to address the issue that a world containing evil seems a malfunction on the part of its creator if indeed that creator possesses perfection. Like Spinoza, Leibniz recognizes the principle of perfection as a reality, yet whereas for Spinoza the best possible world is a product of divine power,

---

[30] Ibid.

for Leibniz, it is a product of divine choice actuated in necessity. For both thinkers the actual world is the best possible one, thus while the path differs substantially the destination in this regard is the same. God as perfect is obligated to create the best possible world, He will to do so, and He in fact does so.
Leibniz' theodicy also relies on plenitude, as demonstrated in part by his deployment of aesthetic illustration of the nature of evil as both necessary and as privation. He says,

> ... to say that the painter is the author of all that is real in the two paintings, without however being the author of what is lacking or the disproportion between the larger and the smaller painting. . . . In effect, what is lacking is nothing more than a simple result of an infallible consequence of that which is positive, without any need for a distinct author [of that which is lacking].[31]

In this case divine authorship is defended against the malfunction claim. Evil has a necessary role in what appears to be a less than ideal world, a role which Leibniz identifies as emerging in three manifestations: (1) metaphysical evil – the degeneration inherent in the limits of the substance(s) of which the world is made, (2) natural evil – the pain and suffering experienced in the world, and (3) moral evil – that which inevitably results in natural evil.[32] Evil, then, completes the picture and is the result of no malfunction at all.

Hume (1711-1776)

---

[31] From *Sämtliche Schriften und Briefe*. (Darmstadt and Berlin: Berlin Academy, 1923), A6.3:151 as quoted in "Leibniz and the Problem of Evil", *Stanford Encyclopedia of Philosophy.*
[32] Susan Neiman, *Evil in Modern Thought* (Princeton, NJ: Princeton University Press, 2004), 22.

Leading up to Hume, theodicy grew to be an increasingly central issue not only in theological discussion but also in philosophical inquiry – for some (such as Leibniz) it was a primary stimulus. Hume's empiricism brought no less emphasis on the topic but did, however, generate dramatically disparate conclusions. Countering in particular the teleological concept, Hume attacks theism mercilessly. While epistemology may be his primary battleground, the problem of evil attracts much of his attention. It is notable that for Hume arriving at a theodicy was not his ambition, rather he sought to obliterate traditional notions of God. Having already countered to his own satisfaction *a priori* arguments for God's existence, Hume attacks what he believes to be the last bastion of grounding for belief in God – the teleological idea.

> If able to demonstrate that God is indifferent to good and evil, He can be made irrelevant and even nonsensical. As a result any theistically based teleological idea would be moot. To accomplish this Hume relies on an ancient iteration of the problem – that of Epicurus. He reminds theists that Epicurus's old questions are yet unanswered. Is he willing to prevent evil, but not able? then he is impotent. Is he able, but not willing? then he is malevolent. Is he both able and willing? whence then is evil?[33]

In Hume's analysis of Epicurus, a more formalized argument begins to take shape. Unless terminology is redefined (as it is in previous theodicies), there are only three possibilities: (1) God is not omnipotent, (2) God is not omnibenevolent, (3) evil does not exist.

---

[33] David Hume, *Dialogues Concerning Natural Religion: The Posthumous Essays on the Immortality of The Soul and Suicide*, Richard Popkin, ed., (Hackett Publishing, 1980), 63.

Hume will not allow any redefinition of evil, as in his *Dialogues Concerning Natural Religion*[34] he lists a number of moral and natural evils which are painfully evident to all. In so doing he concludes against a cosmos initiated by either concern for its creatures or by divine volition, saying:

> Were all living creatures incapable of pain, or were the world administered by particular volitions, evil never could have found access into the universe: and were animals endowed with a large stock of powers and faculties, beyond what strict necessity requires; or were the several springs and principles of the universe so accurately framed as to preserve always the just temperament and medium; there must have been very little ill in comparison of what we feel at present. What then shall we pronounce on this occasion?[35]

Once *a priori* ideas of inherent goodness are vanquished (theistic or otherwise) such goodness can only be derived from experience, and Hume has an easy time of dismissing that possibility:

> But let us still assert, that as this goodness is not antecedently established, but must be inferred from the phenomena, there can be no grounds for such an inference, while there are so many ills in the universe, and while these ills might so easily have been remedied, as far as human understanding can be allowed to judge on such a subject.[36]

Having established the groundlessness of the idea of teleological goodness, Hume closes the issue with a resounding indictment derived from simple observation:

---

[34] Section 11, in particular.
[35] David Hume, *Dialogues Concerning Natural Religion*, Section 11:8.
[36] Ibid.

> But inspect a little more narrowly these living existences, the only beings worth regarding. How hostile and destructive to each other! How insufficient all of them for their own happiness! How contemptible or odious to the spectator! The whole presents nothing but the idea of a blind Nature, impregnated by a great vivifying principle, and pouring forth from her lap, without discernment or parental care, her maimed and abortive children![37]

As representative of Hume, these statements fasten theological conceptions of evil and notions of the character of God to theories of knowledge, and they additionally raise questions of the nature of good which leads further into ethical discussions. For Hume, theology and philosophy are too connected, and he wishes to extricate philosophical inquiry from the grips unverifiable religious notions. Insofar as this is his objective, Hume becomes perhaps the lead protagonist for theodicy. Any attempt at theodicy which does not at least consider the colossal issues he raises will be found deficient or partial at best.

Kant (1724-1804)

In contrast to Hume, Kant sought to extrapolate systematic order in the cosmos. Like Hume, his epistemological grounding necessitated certain conclusions – while Hume's empiricism supplied an a priori opposition to the metaphysical, Kant's structuralism furnished a means for explaining the existence of evil in a manner not fully incompatible with a theistic outlook. For Kant *radical evil* is self-inflicted on those who *will* corruptly. Kant's metaphysical conception of radical evil relates directly to his deontological ethics. Connection can likewise be drawn from the basic issues of theodicy to moral duty in Kant, thus generating a point of intersection between

---

[37] Ibid., 11:9.

metaphysics and ethics. If evil for Kant is such a pivotal issue, then how does he account for its presence?

> We shall say, therefore, of the character (good or evil) distinguishing man from other possible rational beings, that it is innate in him. Yet in doing so we shall ever take the position that nature is not to bear the blame (if it is evil) or take the credit (if it is good), but that man himself is its author.[38]

Evil is not divinely inspired but rather is intrinsic within the person and inextricably connected to the utilization of free choice. Kant continues:

> To have a good or an evil disposition as an inborn natural constitution does not here mean that it has not been acquired by the man who harbors it, that he is not author of it, but rather, that it has not been acquired in time (that he has always been good, or evil, from his youth up). The disposition, i.e., the ultimate subjective ground of the adoption of maxims, can be one only and applies universally to the whole use of freedom. Yet this disposition itself must have been adopted by free choice, for otherwise it could not be imputed.[39]

Whereas Kant attributes the existence of evil within human character to the (corrupt) deployment of free choice, he acknowledges three distinct degrees of evil: (1) frailty of human nature, (2) impurity of the human heart, and (3) wickedness of the human heart – the propensity toward evil. Evil is found to differing degree universally within human nature – so much so, in fact, that Kant says it is "woven into human nature."[40] As

---

[38] Immanuel Kant, *Religion Within the Limits of Reason Alone*, Book 1, Section 15.
[39] Ibid.
[40] Ibid.

such, to become free from evil is the "greatest prize,"[41] and to fail to be such is man's own fault. In deriving such conclusions Kant relies on two theodical components: (1) free will as source of origin and causation of evil, and (2) the principle of plenitude. In his representation of the latter, Kant reckons the end game as the establishment of an ethical commonwealth – the founding of a kingdom of God on earth. As free choice plays an important role in this, evil is a necessity in this drama.

Conclusion

From a synthesis of historical views on the problem of evil from the presocratic through the modern era, two primary definitions emerge: one, elucidated primarily in medieval theology from a monotheistic vantage point, revolves around harmonizing the concurrent existences of God and evil; and the second, from presocratic and modern naturalistic grounding, centers on the question of whether the cosmos is teleological. Whether from aesthetic motivation or otherwise – the question of teleology persists.

The iteration of the problem from a monotheistic perspective is dependent upon three perfections attributed to God: omniscience, omnipotence, and omnibenevolence. If any one of the three fail, then God (as defined) cannot exist. The existence of evil seems to threaten at any time at least one of these perfections. The problem, then, as gleaned from historical thinkers could be formally structured as follows:

> Premise 1: If G is X then G is A (If God is existent then God is omniscient)

---

[41] Ibid., Book 3, Section 85.

The History of the Problem of Evil 181

Premise 2: If G is X then G is B (If God is existent then God is omnipotent)
Premise 3: If G is X then G is C (If God is existent then God is omnibenevolent)
Premise 4: If D is X then G is not A (If evil is existent then God is not omniscient)
Premise 5: If D is X then G is not B (If evil is existent then God is not omnipotent)
Premise 6: If D is X then G is not C (If evil is existent then God is not omnibenevolent)
Premise 7: D is X (evil is existent)
Conclusion: G is not X (God is not existent)

Given the positive truth value of the premises, the conclusion necessarily follows. This obviously creates a very significant theological conundrum which can only be resolved if it can be shown that any one of the premises is false.

If Premise 1 is false, then omniscience is *not* prerequisite to the existence of God. God theoretically could possess omnipotence and omnibenevolence and yet lack omniscience, the lacking of which allows for the existence of evil without logically nullifying His existence. In this case, God is powerful enough to eliminate evil, and he is morally perfect enough to want it eliminated, but He does not have the knowledge either that it exists, or of how it should be eliminated. If Premise 2 is false, then God has the necessary knowledge and the desire to eliminate evil but lacks the power to do so. If Premise 3 is false, then God has both the knowledge and the power to eliminate evil but does not desire to do so. If Premises 4, 5, or 6 is false, then the existence of evil does not constitute a contradiction to one or more of the perfections asserted of God. If Premise 7 is false, then there is no problem at all, since evil is non-existent.

From a naturalistic perspective, and independent of theological considerations, the second permutation of the problem discusses the plausibility of good, order, and ultimately purpose within the cosmos despite apparent contradictions brought by suffering within nature, for example, and relies on the same basic logical structure. Such a problem could be formalized in the following manner:

> Premise 1: If N is P then N is G (If nature is purposed then nature is good)
> Premise 2: If N is P then N is O (If nature is purposed then nature is orderly)
> Premise 3: If S is R then N is not G (If suffering is a reality then nature is not good)
> Premise 4: If S is R then N is not O (If suffering is a reality then nature is not orderly)
> Premise 5: S is R (suffering is a reality)
> Conclusion: N is not P (nature is not purposed)

As evidenced from a historical overview and resultant definitions, the problem of the existence of evil has confounded theologian and philosopher alike and is not isolated exclusively within either category of thought. Insomuch as it is true that both disciplines must confront the issue, it seems that at least two considerations should be made.

First, a working definition of the problem from each standpoint (such as those here provided) should be perceived. Any problem to be resolved requires at least general agreement on the part of the participants regarding core definitions. And while I am not suggesting that the definitions offered here necessarily provide finality in this regard, I do suggest that these particular formulations, derived from the problem as historically iterated, provide a reduction of terms apt to facilitate comparative analysis of proposed solutions, rendering more readily visible presuppositions and other such factors which would significantly impact conclusions. In short, a definition extracted from a plurality of theorists addressing the problem over time will allow for broader and even interdisciplinary critique, thus deepening the analysis.

Second, as this kind of analysis takes place a reduced-term definition provides greater opportunity for interdisciplinary testing of ideas. Philosophical attempts at resolving the issue – or reframing the issue so as not to require resolution – when held to the light (or darkness) of theology must meet challenges it might not otherwise wish to consider. The core premises of naturalistic philosophy may be examined in this context, and in light of such testing will either be shown to want further refinement or will be strengthened even further in its convictions. Likewise, theological efforts, when informed by naturalistic argument, must question its very basis of authority. Is it grounded properly? Is it hermeneutically sound? The testing which philosophical inquiry brings provides opportunity for heightened precision which might not be otherwise motivated. The informing of one discipline by the other, then, gives occasion for strengthening or dismissal of views as the case may demand.

With these two considerations in view, and in light of the historical inquiry and the problem's ramifications for epistemology, metaphysics, ethics, and aesthetics, there may be perhaps no more fertile ground for interdisciplinary inquiry between philosophy and theology than the problem of evil.

184 The Sofa Rule

20
Aesthetics and the Problem of Evil

Where do theology and philosophy intersect, and at what points can they be observed as doing so? For Aquinas, theology was a subset of philosophy – a part, actually. He describes the relationship saying,

> ...all things which "are" are dealt with in the philosophical sciences, which treat even of God, wherefore one part of philosophy is called theology, or the science of divine things...[1]

But is this assertion of proximity justified? If yes, then the further question may arise as to whether or not theology need be relegated to mere component of philosophy, or whether it is deserving of higher billing. The latter question will go unanswered here, for the task at hand will be limited in scope to arguing in favor of Aquinas' assertion of interconnectedness, even though I would not find his organizing hierarchy to be fully adequate.

---

[1] Thomas Aquinas, *On Nature and Grace*, A.M. Fairweather, ed., (Philadelphia, PA: Westminster Press, 1954), 35.

For purposes of the discussion here, the theological-philosophical connection will be discussed in the realm of aesthetics, and specifically so in the context of the problem of evil as it relates to both disciplines. In short, the problem of evil provides a point of entry for both philosophical and theological inquiry, impacting several aspects of both disciplines, of which aesthetics will be the focal point here.

What is the Problem of Evil?

Epicurus is generally credited with uncovering the problem, as evidenced by Lactantius' polemic against Epicurus' findings:

> What happiness, then, can there be in God, if He is always inactive, being at rest and un-moveable? if He is deaf to those who pray to Him, and blind to His worshippers? [lacking omniscience] What is so worthy of God, and so befitting to Him, as providence? [lacking omnipotence] But if He cares for nothing [lacking omnibenevolence], and foresees nothing, He has lost all His divinity [note: Epicurus' necessary conclusion]. What else does he say, who takes from God all power and all substance, except that there is no God at all [notes mine]?[2]

And again, he says – in direct response to Epicurus,

> God, says Epicurus, regards nothing [premise 1: lacking omnibenevolence]; therefore He has no power [conclusion: lacking omnipotence]. For he who has power must of necessity regard affairs [premise 2: inferential relationship between omnibenevolence and omnipotence]. For if He has power, and does not use it, what so great cause is there that, I will not say our race, but even the universe itself, should be contemptible in His sight [notes mine]?[3]

---

[2] Lanctantius, *On the Anger of God.*
[3] Ibid.

From Lactantius' comments, Epicurus' trilemma can be deduced. Hume later states the problem in simple form, offering an excellent base for defining the problem. Hume says,

> Epicurus's old questions are yet unanswered. Is he willing to prevent evil, but not able? then he is impotent. Is he able, but not willing? then he is malevolent. Is he both able and willing? whence then is evil?[4]

The problem of evil revolves around certain assumed perfections in the character of God, that seem to be contradictory to observed reality – specifically the reality of evil. While Epicurus deals with the incompatibility of each of the three perfections (omniscience, omnipotence, omnibenevolence) with the existence of evil, Hume simplifies the issue, focusing on only two horns of the dilemma – namely the incompatibility of omnipotence and omnibenevolence with the existence of evil, yet the more complex form is more useful for purposes here, since it presents the problem in more complete form. The more complex form of the argument can be framed in propositional form as follows:

> Premise 1: If G is X then G is A (If God is existent then God is omniscient)
> Premise 2: If G is X then G is B (If God is existent then God is omnipotent)
> Premise 3: If G is X then G is C (If God is existent then God is omnibenevolent)

---

[4] David Hume, *Dialogues Concerning Natural Religion: The Posthumous Essays on the Immortality of the Soul and Suicide*, Richard Popkin, ed., (Hackett Publishing, 1980), 63.

Premise 4: If D is X then G is not A (If evil is existent then God is not omniscient)
Premise 5: If D is X then G is not B (If evil is existent then God is not omnipotent)
Premise 6: If D is X then G is not C (If evil is existent then God is not omnibenevolent)
Premise 7: D is X (evil is existent)
Conclusion: G is not X (God is not existent)

Given the positive truth value of the premises, the conclusion necessarily follows. This obviously creates a very significant theological conundrum which can only be resolved if it can be shown that any one of the premises is false.

If Premise 1 is false, then omniscience is *not* prerequisite to the existence of God. God theoretically could possess omnipotence and omnibenevolence and yet lack omniscience, the lacking of which allows for the existence of evil without logically nullifying His existence. In this case, God is powerful enough to eliminate evil, and he is morally perfect enough to want it eliminated, but He does not have the knowledge either that it exists, or of how it should be eliminated. If Premise 2 is false, then God has the necessary knowledge and the desire to eliminate evil but lacks the power to do so. If Premise 3 is false, then God has both the knowledge and the power to eliminate evil but does not desire to do so. If Premises 4, 5, or 6 is false, then the existence of evil does not constitute a contradiction to one or more of the perfections asserted of God. If Premise 7 is false, then there is no problem at all, since evil is non-existent.

Theodicy, then, will rely upon the faultiness of one or more of the premises. It is beyond the scope of this present discussion to deal with proposed theodicies, rather the matter at hand is to demonstrate that this is not a purely theological issue, but that instead it extends deeply into the philosophical realm.

How is the Problem of Evil a Philosophical Problem?

As a foundational principle in his ontological argument for the existence of God, Anselm argues that existence is a necessary element of perfection. His argument is as follows:

> ...certainly that greater than which cannot be understood cannot exist only in thought, for if it exists only in thought it could also be thought of as existing in reality as well, which is greater. If, therefore, that than which greater cannot be thought exists in thought alone, then that than which greater cannot be thought turns out to be that than which something greater actually can be thought, but that is obviously impossible. Therefore something than which greater cannot be thought undoubtedly exists both in thought and in reality.[5]

Closely akin to Anselm's assertion of the importance of existence is the notion of plenitude, the idea that in order for the universe to possess perfection it must also be necessarily *full*. Leibniz describes this as follows:

> ...there is obtained as great variety as possible, along with the greatest possible order; that is to say, it is the way to get as much perfection as possible...[6]

The greatest possible variety is the only way to achieve the greatest degree of perfection, and thus for Leibniz, the best possible world is one which must of necessity contain evil, but would contain as little as is necessary and as little as is possible. His idea of nature as a plenum which then connects the variety (and possibility) resulting in a sweeping sort of cause and effect. He describes it thusly:

---

[5] Anselm, *Proslogion*, David Barr, (trans.), Ch. 2.
[6] G.W. Leibniz, *The Monadology*, Robert Latta (trans.), 58.

> For all is a plenum (and thus all matter is connected together) and in the plenum every motion has an effect upon distant bodies in proportion to their distance, so that each body not only is affected by those which are in contact with it and in some way feels the effect of everything that happens to them, but also is mediately affected by bodies adjoining those with which it itself is in immediate contact. Wherefore it follows that this intercommunication of things extends to any distance, however great.[7]

Plenitude, for Leibniz, is a theodicy based on necessity and possibility, and can be simply elucidated as follows: all that can be is, and what is, is the very best that can be. This principle – even if it can be shown to be a failed theodicy – still demonstrates the interrelationship between philosophy and theology.

Charles Nussbaum sums up plenitude as providing that "...the evil in the world is a necessary ingredient in the world's overall perfection or degree of reality."[8] But for Nussbaum there is present an additional aspect which draws, in itself, a connection between the two disciplines, as this aspect places the problem of evil squarely on the philosophical doorstep: he views plenitude as a theodicy and asserts that the principle of plenitude is aesthetically motivated.[9]

Regarding metaphysical cosmology, Nussbaum underscores three perspectives on dealing with the opposing ideas of necessity and contingency: (1) Spinoza, as operating within a modal framework – emphasizing strict causal determinism – the present world is from necessity due to His omnipotence, and is not a matter of divine choice; (2) Descartes

---

[7] Ibid., 61.
[8] Charles Nussbaum, "Aesthetics and the Problem of Evil," in *Metaphilosophy*, Vol. 34, No. 3, April 2003.
[9] Ibid.

as representing a teleological framework, on the underlying premise that God's will provides the origin of provenance of laws of nature, and since based upon God's will, they (laws of all kinds) could have been different had he willed it so, yet due to moral perfections of God the best possible world has been chosen; and (3) Leibniz as representing a mediatory approach, combining elements of necessity and contingency – even though God, due to moral perfections must act for the best[necessity], there remains opportunity for choice within the framework of a divine teleology [contingency].

Nussbaum suggests that, while Leibniz and Descartes offer theodicies here (Spinoza's does not, as his definition of evil is more akin to a secondary quality than a primary one), these fall short because they belong to a tradition of explanatory rationalism which attempts "to accomplish what only a type of art and perhaps revealed religion can accomplish: the complete rationalization of its object."[10] But from whence comes this desire for 'thoroughgoing intelligibility'? Elsewhere Nussbaum cites Pascal's concern regarding the possibility of life's meaninglessness as the grounding for not only of religious belief, but also of "elaborate metaphysical cosmologies like those of Spinoza and Hegel that purport either to eliminate contingency as an illusion, or to subflate (*aufheben*) it into necessity."[11] While it is perhaps quite clear how the opposing of contingency could impact religion, resulting in certain metaphysical conclusions, how is it that aesthetics is also so influenced?

---

[10] Ibid.
[11] Charles O. Nussbaum, *The Musical Representation: Meaning, Ontology, and Emotion* (Cambridge, MA: The MIT Press, 2007), 260.

In the World as Art

Kant associates the perceiving of order in nature with the feeling of aesthetic pleasure. He says in his *Third Critique*:

> The conceived harmony of nature in the manifold of its particular laws with our need of finding universality of principles for it must, so far as our insight goes, be deemed contingent, but withal indispensable for the requirements of our understanding, and, consequently, a finality by which nature is in accord with our aim…[12]

That aim being pleasure, nature's finality is seen, in one sense, as teleological, and quite important to our own understanding of it. For Kant, art is production through freedom.[13] But it is also one that is formulated by rational deliberation and not mere instinct. A Kantian bit of humor demonstrates, at least, that art is purposed:

> If, as sometimes happens, in a search through a bog, we light on a piece of hewn wood, we do not say it is a product of nature but of art. Its producing cause had an end in view to which the object owes its from. Apart from such cases, we recognize an art in everything formed in such a way that its actuality must have been preceded by a representation of the thing in its cause…[14]

For Kant, art is purposed by way of rational deliberation yet is enjoyed aesthetically when it brings pleasure unrelated to utility or (perhaps) even telos. But for the perceiver of art to enjoy art in a properly aesthetic way, the perceiver must rightly reckon the object as belonging to the proper category that is art.

---

[12] Immanuel Kant, *The Critique of Judgment, Part I*, James Creek Meredith, trans. (Stillwell, KS: Digireads, 2005), 19.
[13] Ibid., 89.
[14] Ibid., 89-90.

While Kant distinguishes between nature and art, environmental aestheticians Carlson and Berleant assert that appreciation for the natural world should (and can) be as "emotionally and as cognitively rich as is that of art."[15]

This perspective is not a novel one, as it is reflected by many in theistic circles as well. As goes the first stanza of Babcock's 1901 hymn, "This is My Father's World:"

> This is my Father's world
> And to my listening ears
> All nature sings, and round me rings
> The music of the spheres

Nineteenth century English poet Philip James Bailey notably asserted that "Art is a man's nature; nature is God's art," and nearly three thousand years before Bailey or Babcock, the Israelite King David describes the telos of nature in Psalm 19:

> The heavens are telling of the glory of God;
> And their expanse is declaring the work of His hands.
> Day to day pours forth speech,
> And night to night reveals knowledge.

There is no shortage of evidence that throughout history, nature has been perceived quite regularly as, at least in some form, divine art. And despite Kant's differentiation between nature and art, it is asserted in theistic traditions that nature is both possessing telos and formulation by rational deliberation. It is this rationally devised telos which Pascal was seeking. This is the root of plenitude utilized by Descartes Spinoza and Leibniz.

---

[15] Allen Carlson and Arnold Berleant, Eds., *The Aesthetics of Natural Environments* (Canada: Broadview Press, 2004), 15.

It is against this backdrop that Nussbaum argues contrary to plenitude as having anything but aesthetic or religious motivation, saying,

> ...there are no longer any grounds to claim that the cosmos is perfect or even "excellent"...for without the principle of plenitude and Spinoza's allegedly self-evidently true axioms and self-evidently acceptable definitions, such judgments have no basis.[16]

If the perfect or excellent cosmos has indeed perished, then what remains is not teleologically intelligible, and such things as suffering, for example, cannot be seen then as the product of design. Describing the art of the tragedy, Nussbaum says

> ...the hallmark of tragedy is a certain rationalization of suffering, suffering rendered somehow meaningful and understandable. The details all fit in with the whole, the senseless surd is eliminated, and contingency is vanquished by necessity.[17]

It is in this rationalization of suffering that plenitude has an aesthetic appeal. It is also at this point that the problem of evil can begin to be described in less theological terms and take on a more philosophical color. What was previously a trilemma regarding the character of God and the existence of evil can now be connected with the telos of nature and the suffering of its components. Perhaps the problem can now be stated in naturalistic terms as follows:

> Premise 1: If N is P then N is G (If nature is purposed then nature is good)
> Premise 2: If N is P then N is O (If nature is purposed then nature is orderly)

---

[16] Nussbaum, 2003.
[17] Ibid.

Premise 3: If S is R then N is not G (If suffering is a reality then nature is not good)
Premise 4: If S is R then N is not O (If suffering is a reality then nature is not orderly)
Premise 5: S is R (suffering is a reality)
Conclusion: N is not P (nature is not purposed)

As in the theological formulation, the conclusion here follows necessarily from the premises, and plenitude offers a theodical means of explanation – if any premise can be shown to be false, then the argument is invalid.

Premise 1 makes inherent goodness synonymous with purpose. It could be argued that nature is good regardless of whether it is purposed or not. But as previously cited, an argument can be made that nature is not perfect nor is it excellent. On the other hand, the defense of purpose in nature would lie in a more Platonic definition of goodness which would indeed require at least some degree of telos. Premise 2 relies on order as the outflow of purpose. It can be argued that there is no underlying order, and thus no purpose, but yet it cannot be demonstrated that there is a complete absence of order. Premise 3 introduces the variable of suffering, asserting that its presence in nature would constitute a contradiction between the good and the natural. In premise 4 suffering has the same negating impact on order. Premise 5 seems a certain truism, hence the conclusion against the teleological – and against plenitude.

Plenitude, therefore, is a means whereby, as in the form of tragedy, in the realm of naturalistic philosophy suffering can be defined and explained in a way so that purpose in nature is not negated, and in the realm of metaphysical philosophy evil can be defined and explained in such a way so as not to contradict the existence of a certain kind of deity. Plenitude thus serves as a point of contact between philosophy and theology, offering an intersection of both problem and solution.

The Impotence of Theodicy vs. the Explanatory Construct

For Nussbaum, theodicy is inappropriate and ineffective as explanatory of reality as it is based on the flawed grounding of rationalistic metaphysics. His argument strikes perhaps at a more central nerve to present ethical discussions – the reality or non-reality of objective morality. Note Nussbaum's semi-concluding comment:

> Once rationalistic metaphysics and theology lose their grip, we may be less inclined to see the ideal objects of morality (the right and the good) as given or imposed and more inclined to see them as constituted by the practical principles we adopt. In this way, essentialism and theodicy can be said to find their proper places and assume their proper functions as disguised practical ideals...[18]

In this perspective, theodicy is an application of convention. It has a philosophical place in underlying a particular ethical grid and operating as a narrative tool for (e.g.) divine mandate ethics. Thus, for those holding to this perspective, theodicy – by way of plenitude – profoundly imprints ethics and morality by using aesthetic device to ground and proliferate the tradition.

But what if theodicy is not grounded purely in aesthetic motivation? The device of tragedy does not negate the historicity of events which may fit its pattern simply on grounds that they do indeed fit the pattern. Must all tragedy fall into the fictional category because it is tragic? In the case of theodicy, inquiry can be made as to whether or not the parallel to tragic form can be

---

[18] Ibid.

attributed to life imitating art or whether indeed it is vise versa. Either way the aesthetic ties would be undeniable – either as descriptive or prescriptive, and thus the intersection between philosophy and theology would remain intact (not to mention the metaphysical and ethical intersections that can also be recognized here).

But if theodicy can be asserted as more than an instance of mere metaphysical art or ethical art, then the intersection between the two disciplines possesses a heightened fecundity. If this be the case, then theodicy and the principle of plenitude can provide the grounding of a significant source of information. As an explanatory construct a potent theodicy would impact perhaps every area of philosophy. Aesthetics would prove to be just a minor point of contact in light of the impact to be had on metaphysics and ethics, for example. Perhaps most obviously, the right and the good *would* be seen as given, and thus not as conventions. It is likely that this degree of impact is precisely why the interconnectedness between philosophy and theology seems to encounter firm resistance – often from both sides.

In this case, philosophy assigns motivation to theology: namely, seeking aesthetic device to justify ethical mandates. One wonders if philosophy might have its own preconditions on the matter. Guthrie characterizes the rise of philosophy as being related to the presocratics' naturalistic motivation, saying,

> The conviction began to take shape in men's minds that the apparent chaos of events must conceal an underlying order, and that this order is the product of impersonal forces.[19]

---

[19] W.K.C. Guthrie, *The History of Greek Philosophy Vol. I: The earlier Presocratics and the Pythagoreans* (Great Britain: Cambridge University Press, 1962), 26.

Naturalistic motivations cannot be attributed to the presocratics alone, however. Note Wells' characterization of Platonic thinking as

> ...a landmark in this history; it is a new thing in the development of mankind, this appearance of the idea of willfully and completely recasting human conditions. So far mankind has been living by traditions under the fear of the gods. Here is a man [Plato] who says boldly to our race, and as if it were a quite reasonable and natural thing to say, "Take hold of your lives. Most of the things that distress you, you can avoid; most of these things that dominate you, you can overthrow. You can do as you will with them."[20]

In a sense, Plato's explanations of suffering and means of avoidance of the same provide a kind of naturalistic theodicy. Suffering must be explained. It is far too jolting to simply ignore, and if philosophical inquiry were to avoid attending to such an issue, then how could it justify discussion on issues of lesser import? The question then is how does philosophy ground the inquiry regarding the existence of and nature of suffering. It is evident that while theology chooses to ground the dialogue with a metaphysical construct, philosophy generally evades this grounding in favor of a more materialistic one. Whether suffering can be addressed as forming a component of telos or whether it is mere happenstance is a crucial discussion for both disciplines, and if either fails to offer reliable answers one has to wonder of the trustworthiness of the mode of inquiry.

The problem of evil provides not only an example of the pervasive interconnectedness of philosophy and theology in the realms of aesthetics, metaphysics, ethics, etc., but it also

---

[20] H.G. Wells, *The Outline of History, Vol. I* (Garden City, NY: Garden City Books, 1949), 331-332.

provides unique opportunity to lay bare both the motivation and methodology of each course of study.

The Sofa Rule

21
Can God Really Know: The Open Theism Question

The problem of evil presents a challenge for philosophers and theologians who hold to the existence of God. Simply stated, the problem includes three conditional premises and a concluding question: If God is all powerful, all knowing, and all beneficent, then how can evil exist? In order to resolve the problem that the concluding question implies, one of the three premises has to be denied or altered. While I would suggest that the problem can only be resolved by understanding and defining the beneficence of God through the lens of His holiness (as emphasized in Isaiah 6 and Revelation 4), the theology of divine openness, otherwise known as open theism, attempts to answer the question by denying the other two premises. Open theism is on the extreme end of the "free-will" spectrum as a philosophical attempt at resolving the problem.

Clark Pinnock, the preeminent proponent of open theism, presented a lecture at the 2007 Open Theology and Science Conference at Eastern Nazarene College, in which he addressed the issue of why he was an open theist.[1] In that lecture he discusses some of the more salient and foundational points of Open Theism:

> God created the world for love and relations. Genuine love has an element of decision, and requires at least a degree of freedom. Thus genuine love requires risk. God has determined that love is worth the risk. God is involved in the world, rather than detached from it. God participates in human suffering, and makes his actions contingent upon human actions...God could know details of the future, but renounces that in order to provide genuine freedom. God could control the world if he wished, but He does not wish to. God is not ontologically limited, but He voluntarily limits Himself for the sake of relationship, resulting in a kind of voluntary panentheism. In love, God chose general rather than meticulous sovereignty. In order to grant libertarian genuine freedom, God chose to give up complete control. God took risks. Consequently, God does not have an exhaustive knowledge of the future. Instead, He has partnership in history, as senior partner, with humans. The future is not yet formed, but is being made as we go along. God knows what could happen and is prepared for all possibilities...The point is a personal, relational, interactive God, rather than a God of abstract features. God anticipates all that can happen and is prepared for it but corrects unexpected events by means of His own repentance.

In Pinnock's view, open theism is both Biblical and practical, having numerous applications. It corrects hyper-transcendent understandings of God. It contributes to epistemology and science in that it parallels in theology the dynamic cosmology of quantum mechanics. It reflects a world of true becoming, and is also compatible with an evolutionary cosmology.[2] It allows for

---

[1] Clark Pinnock, "Clark Pinnock on Open Theology," Open Theology and Science Conference, Eastern Nazarene College, 2007, viewed at https://www.youtube.com/watch?v=wZo6Q-N5xvY.

[2] https://www.youtube.com/watch?v=l1FLOtyQEro.

divine providence and the interactivity of God, in contrast to the limitations of God's freedom in exhaustive sovereignty. Finally, open theism provides a theodicy, resolving the problem of evil by its assertion that God renounces omniscience, allowing evil, in order to provide genuine freedom, which is required for genuine love.

While open theism possesses some obvious philosophical advantages from the perspective of those who have difficulty with the concept of exhaustive sovereignty, the view is the theological equivalent of Heraclitus' can't-step-twice-in-the-same-river *world of becoming*, in contrast to Parmenides' cue-ball *world of being*. In short, open theism represents a theological iteration of the classic philosophical debate contrasting *being* and *becoming*. The debate is nothing new, but Pinnock's appeal to the Bible as the source of open theism's derivation represents a development as significant as if someone claimed that Heraclitus' cosmology was Biblically derived. The question, then, that we must answer is whether open theism is simply representative of a philosophical theory, or whether it indeed represents the cosmological model of Scripture.

The first Biblical instance in which both God's sovereignty and human responsibility are discussed in the same context is in God's commissioning of Moses and God's prophecy regarding Pharaoh. "I know that the king of Egypt will not permit you to go, except under compulsion."[3] If God foreknew Pharaoh's coming disobedience, and if God's overall purpose is to allow for genuine love and genuine freedom, then any foreknowledge on God's part would represent a restriction of that love and freedom. Thus even the smallest degree of

---

[3] Exodus 3:19.

foreknowledge would violate God's freedom-driven model. While God's discussion of foreknowledge could be arguably passive (responsive) rather than active (causative), there is no arguing that God was indeed active in the restriction of Pharaoh's freedom, as He preannounces that not only does He know what Pharaoh will do but He adds, "...I will harden his heart so that he will not let the people go."[4] The use of the piel (intensive) form of *chazaq* (to harden or strengthen) leaves no doubt as to the level of God's activeness in this.

Further, it is notable that this prophecy precedes all ten plagues, otherwise referred to as judgments against Egypt[5] and against all the gods of Egypt.[6] Also, as the plagues near their conclusion, God reiterates twice that he would again harden Pharaoh's heart,[7] and in both instances the piel stem is used – emphasizing the intensive quality of God's activity. It is fatal to open theism that God had foreknowledge and also exercised His sovereignty on Pharaoh in such a way that caused God's judgment to come upon the whole land of Egypt. Such a maneuver is certainly not compatible with the theory that God restricts His own sovereignty in order to foster love through freedom. The purpose for God's hardening of Pharaoh is explicitly stated in His preannouncement: "that I may multiply My signs and My wonders in the land of Egypt."[8] This reflects a doxological teleology, not a panentheistic or relational one. God's purpose is His glory, not simply love or relationship. God would be honored through Pharaoh and all His army[9] – which was

---

[4] 4:21.
[5] 7:4.
[6] 12:12.
[7] 14:4,17.
[8] 7:3, 14:4.
[9] 14:4.

great for the Egyptians, who would learn that Yahweh was God, but it didn't work out so well for Pharaoh or his army. Or for the firstborn in Egypt who lost their lives due to Pharaoh's hard heart.

Finally, we discover in the Exodus episodes that as the events unfold, five times we are told that the Lord hardened Pharaoh's heart,[10] five times Pharaoh's heart was hardened,[11] and three times Pharaoh hardened his own heart.[12] In four of the five passive references, the verses conclude with "as the Lord had said,"[13] indicating that the hardening of Pharaoh's heart in these instances was part of God's active hardening of Pharaoh's heart. These occurrences show that God was completely sovereign over the situation, for the purpose of expressing His own character and glory, and that not only was Pharaoh held accountable for his hardness of heart, but so were the animals, the people, the armies, and the gods of Egypt. As Paul later explains, there is no injustice with God, even when He limits the freedom of an individual by hardening them for His own purposes.[14]

The Exodus episodes debunk open theism's key premise that God's cosmology is purposed in relationship and requires the restriction of His sovereignty so as not to impinge on the human freedom necessary for genuine love. If even in one instance the premise is contradicted, then the entire model (as a universal cosmology) fails. Of course, there are many other passages that are problematic for open theism (which we would

---

[10] 9:12, 10:1,20,27, 11:10, 14:8.
[11] 7:13, 22, 8:19, 9:7,35.
[12] 8:15, 8:32, 9:35.
[13] 7:13,22, 8:15,19.
[14] Romans 9:14-18.

expect if it is not compatible with the Biblical model), but the Exodus narrative is enough evidence to expose open theism as a philosophically and not Biblically derived theological concept. Further, open theism so misrepresents God, His word, and His activities as to be barely recognizable as honoring Him as God at all. Next we look at how roughly forty other passages answer open theism.

Other Passages Answer Clark Pinnock's Open Theism

Genesis 6:6 – God is sorry, and grieves. The LXX uses the word *enthumeomai*, which is simply to consider or think about, not to "be sorry" (see Mt 1:20). The Hebrew *nachem* is to have sorrow or to console oneself. Clearly God has emotional responses to the deeds of men. Still this give no indication of what God did or did not know beforehand. If He wants to have foreknowledge and still be saddened by what takes place, does He not have the right to do that? Or is He only allowed to express emotion if He follows the rules of open theism?

Genesis 8:1, 9:15-16 (and Ex 6:5) – God's remembering, is not indicative of His otherwise forgetting. Rather it points to a return to focus of that which is remembered. God didn't forget Noah, nor the covenant. To assume that God's remembering requires His first forgetting, demands the presupposition that God has the same limitations as humanity. To use God's remembering as an argument that He forgets or does not know, requires presupposing that the premise of open theism is correct before examining the Biblical data.

Genesis 11:5, 18:20-21 – references to the Lord physically relocating typically refers to the second Person of the Trinity. To "go down and see" would not indicate any limitation of that second Person's sovereignty or knowledge, but rather would be consistent with the second Person's existing in a physical form as in the cases when referred to as the angel of the Lord.

Genesis 22:12 – the angel of the Lord is here the second Person of the Trinity (compare Gen 22:11, 15, and 16). "For I now know" is not a statement of divine ignorance, but rather the opposite, nor does it require that He did not have the knowledge previously. Note the contrast between Romans 4 (Abraham's justification before God) and James 2 (Abraham's justification before himself and others).

Genesis 50:20 – God intended not just the outcome, but the activity itself.

Exodus 32:14 – here God "changes His mind." The LXX uses the word *ilasthe*, which is passive for appease – He was appeased about the harm He was going to do. Clearly He did not intend to destroy the people and start over with Moses – that would have been a direct violation of other promises He had made (e.g., His promise regarding Judah's royal future). Once again, it appears He is testing Moses to allow Moses an opportunity to trust in the promises of God. Moses passes the test.

Numbers 23:19 – God doesn't lie (LXX, *diartethenai*) or repent as a man, Heb, *wayyitnachem* – in the Hithpael, which is intensively reflexive: be intensely sorry *of or for Himself*. God can change His mind, or He can grieve, but He doesn't do either as a man would. He is distinct in His ways.[15]

Deuteronomy 13:3 describes that God is testing Israel through false prophets in order to know (Heb, *leda'at*, LXX, *eidenai*). The verb *to know* is in the infinitive in both Hebrew and the Greek of the Septuagint, and is active, meaning God is

---

[15] Isaiah 55:8-9.

the one doing the knowing. This is the same lexical root and type of context as that of Genesis 22:12. In the Genesis instance we have New Testament commentary that helps us understand that the test was actually for Abraham, and involved justification before himself and others, not before God (Rom 4, Jam 2). Deuteronomy 13:3 is not referenced in the New Testament, so there is not an explicit explanation regarding whether or not God had prior knowledge in this instance. However, God knew His plans to cut off the nations who could corrupt Israel,[16] and that Israel would be corrupted if Israel followed after their ways,[17] and He knew that they would indeed follow after their ways and reap the consequences.[18] In light of these various expressions of knowledge, it appears that *to know* in 13:3 carries the weight of *to demonstrate* or to *know by experience*, rather than *to know* as a contrast to having uncertainty.

1 Samuel 15:35 – God regretted, consoled, or was sorry (*nicham*). This shows an emotional response, with no indication that God did not previously know the outcome. It is notable that Saul was of the tribe of Benjamin, though God had made a promise regarding Judah as the tribe of royalty.[19] Just as God could not have destroyed the nation and started over with Moses, He would not have given Saul a preeminent kingdom, as Saul was not from the royal tribe.

Psalm 44:21 and 139:1, 23-24 – God is ever aware of what goes on in the inner man. Psalm 139:16 – David's days ordained before the first one began. Proverbs 16:1,9 – God's sovereignty

---

[16] Deuteronomy 12:29.
[17] 12:30.
[18] 28:45, 29:4, 30:1.
[19] Genesis 49:10.

trumps human planning. Isaiah 41:22-23 – knowledge of the future was a litmus test God required to determine whether or not gods were legitimate or false (see also Deut 18:21-22).

Jeremiah 7:31, 19:5, 32:35 – it didn't enter His mind or heart (*leb*) that they should (prescriptive) do this abomination. He didn't prescribe it. The passage doesn't say He never would have thought of it, in fact, He did know that Israel would break His covenant. See Leviticus 18:21, Deuteronomy 15:4 and 15:11, 18:10, and Deuteronomy 28.

Jeremiah 18:6-8 – provides the formula for how good would operate, and under what conditions He would relent concerning prophesied judgment: if the nation turns from evil. God is sovereign, He holds nations accountable, giving them a choice. God's sovereignty and human choice are not mutually exclusive, because God's sovereignty trumps human choice (e.g., Rom 9:16).

Joel 2:13-14 – this passage references God's "relenting from evil" (*wanichem al harah*). God's relenting (same root term as in Num 23:19 and 1 Sam 15:35) is conditional, as evidenced by His grace. He states consequences to actions, but just as in human salvation, He provides mercy in some cases so the consequences can be avoided. How that mercy is dispensed is up to Him, and not man.[20]

Amos 7:1-6 – in context the two instances of God changing His mind (*nicham*) about executing the judgments He had described, appears more volitional than emotional, but either way, God demonstrates compassion for Jacob, being gracious in judging the nation.[21] In these instances God responds to Amos' prayer. That God responds to prayer is not an indicator one way

---

[20] Romans 9:16.
[21] Amos 7:2,5.

or the other that God does or does not foreknow outcomes, nor is it an indicator that He does not have power over those outcomes.[22] Jonah 4:2 describes an identical situation to Amos 7:1-6.

Mark 13:32 – Jesus admits incomplete knowledge of the future. At the time of His statement, Jesus does not know the hour of His return. However, by the time of the Upper Room Discourse, the disciples acknowledge He knows all, and He accepts that statement without correction.[23] After Jesus' resurrection Peter reiterates the claim that Jesus' knew all things,[24] and again, Jesus did not correct the statement. It appears that Jesus may have temporarily self-restricted His knowledge, as a part of His submission to the Father,[25] and as a part of His humility.

Luke 2:52 – clearly, Jesus grew as a man. It appears that His emptying Himself[26] involved a humbling[27] and a temporary giving up of His glory. That His knowledge was apparently self-restricted would help account for His ability to grow in wisdom and for His temporarily incomplete knowledge of the future.[28] John 2:24-25 – even early in His earthly ministry, Jesus knew all men, and knew what was in man. John 6:64, 70-71, 10:28-29, 13:18-19; 17:12 – Jesus' foreknowledge included who would believe and who wouldn't and who would betray Him, thus restricting the freedom of those He foreknew (including Judas).

---

[22] E.g., James 5:16.
[23] John 16:30.
[24] John 21:17.
[25] Philippians 2:7ff.
[26] Ibid.
[27] 2:8.
[28] Mark 13:32.

Acts 4:27-28 – God predestined the acts of Herod, Pilate, the Gentiles and Israel (incidentally, those labels cover every human on the planet at the time), at least in the context of the rejection and crucifixion of Christ. If one were to argue that genuine freedom were necessary in order for there to be genuine love, then it would be difficult for that argument to deal with the fact of God's predestining work in this most central of events – an event in which all parties involved were held accountable. Perhaps the only exception was those actually crucifying Him, on whose behalf He asked for forgiveness due to their ignorance of the gravity of the situation.[29]

Romans 1:24-27 – God gave them over, they engaged in actions as a result. Whether His giving them over was a result of their rebellion or not does not contradict the reality that God limited their actions (and thus, their freedom) post-rebellion.

Ephesians 1:11 – after describing in depth the significance of the Father's predestining work, Paul adds that He "works all things after the counsel of His will." The Greek word is *panta* – all.

1 Timothy 2:4 – who all men He wills (present active indicative) to have been saved (aorist passive infinitive) and into knowledge of the truth to have come (aorist active infinitive). Also, different word for *desires* than that use in 2 Peter 3:9 (*boulomenos*, in 1 Pet 3:9, *thelei* in 1 Tim 2:4). In their contexts the words have different weight, just as *will* has a different weight than *desire*. God in His sovereignty doesn't always allow Himself what He wants (e.g., Mt 26:29, Jesus uses the same word as that used in 2 Tim 2:4, not the word used in 2 Pet 3:9).

---

[29] Luke 23:34.

Hebrews 4:13 – this verse is talking about Christ Himself (note the pronoun), and observes that all things (*panta*) are open and laid bare before Him.

2 Peter 3:19– the Lord is patient "toward you." The "you" are believers (see 1:1 and 3:1), as He will that none should perish. Similar language to John 10:28. None who are His will perish. Peter reiterates Jesus' words. There is no chance of God's will being thwarted here. Further, the wish for all to come to repentance: repentance is an aorist, thus completed action is referenced without any reference to time. Those who will not perish, have come to repentance, and they are the "you" whom Peter is addressing.

1 John 3:20 – even when our hearts make determinations about our perceptions of reality, God is greater than our hearts, and *His perceptions* are reality.

Conclusion

God thinks differently than humanity does,[30] even if there are occasional similarities. He is holy, holy, holy.[31] Open theism places an anthropomorphic burden on God, presupposing that He is limited in the same ways as is man, and thus cannot be totally sovereign while allowing whatever degree of human volition and responsibility He deems appropriate. Paul's doxology in Romans 11:33-36 serves well enough to remind us that God does not share our limitations, and thus we cannot use an anthropomorphic grid to try to discern the mysteries of His working.

---

[30] Isaiah 55:8-9.
[31] Isaiah 6:3, Revelation 4:8.

22
Breaking the Hinge in the Free-Will vs. Sovereignty Debate

One simple premise undergirds the ideas that either humanity has free volition or that God is sovereign, and that ultimately the two concepts are mutually exclusive. That premise is the hinge upon which the argument turns, favoring either human freedom or Divine sovereignty. Montague Brown illustrates the premise with the following statement:

> The issue of free choice also plays a critical role in that other vexed philosophical puzzle—the problem of evil. For if we do not have free choice, we are not to be blamed or praised for our actions; rather, it is all God's doing. God becomes responsible for moral evil, either by causing it Himself or by punishing us who are not responsible for it.[1]

We can formalize Brown's statement as follows:

> If not FC (free choice), then not A (accountability).

---

[1] Montague Brown, "Augustine on Freedom and God" in *St. Anselm Journal* 2.2 (Spring, 2005): 50.

If not A, then GR (God responsible for evil).

The first stated premise is simply that if there is not free choice, then there is not accountability. The assumed premise is that free choice is required in order for someone to be accountable. The second stated premise is that if there is not accountability, then God is responsible for moral evil. To complete the syllogism, the conclusion is not stated here, but is rather assumed: God being responsible for moral evil would be a bad thing, and we can't have that. So working backwards, we can't have the absence of condition A, thus we can't have the absence of condition FC. The assumed premise is the hinge upon which the argument stands: *moral responsibility requires that human beings perform their actions freely, and not under any coercion.*

Thomas Aquinas echoes the premise when he asserts that, "Man has free-will: "otherwise counsels, exhortations, commands, prohibitions, rewards, and punishments would be in vain."[2] The idea being assumed is that justice in God's judgment requires that humanity made the choice for what it is being judged.

Augustine is comfortable with "a biblical compatibilism between human free will and divine power over the human heart…the two are not in conflict…this is a both/and proposition."[3] In Augustine's view, God works within the human heart in response to chosen sin, either to allow more sin as a penal consequence for original sin, which is in line with justice, or to show grace, which is in line with mercy. Aquinas' understanding is similar:

---

[2] Thomas Aquinas, *Summa Theologicae*, Question 83, Article 1.
[3] Philip Carey, *Inner Grace: Augustine and the Traditions of Plato and Paul* (Oxford: Oxford University Press, 2008), 115.

> And just as by moving natural causes He does not prevent their acts being natural, so by moving voluntary causes He does not deprive their actions of being voluntary: but rather is He the cause of this very thing in them; for He operates in each thing according to its own nature.[4]

The idea that God operates "in each thing according to its own nature" works well within the context of sin, as described in Romans 1, for example. As one follows the sequence considered in Romans 1:18-32, it is evident that there is a giving-over to continued (and perhaps deepening) sin as a consequence of initial rejection. However, if ultimately all are guilty of sin through Adam (as is affirmed in Romans 5:12), then God's intervention "while we were still helpless"[5] and "while we were dead in our transgressions"[6] is not reflective of Him working in each thing according to its nature, but rather Him working to *change* – or dare I say, *violate* – the very nature of the thing in which He is working. If human free will in choosing sin is required for God's justice in judging it, then a requisite degree of human free will in rejecting sin is required in order to receive mercy.

Roger Olson states well the problem implied in these suppositions:

> If we do not have power of contrary choice, then our salvation is not a gift but a fate imposed and others' damnation is not truly deserved. If there is no such thing as libertarian free will, as Edwards argued, then Adam and Eve's fall into sin was part of the plan of God, controlled by God, and makes God a moral monster. If salvation is not something freely chosen or freely rejected, then,

---

[4] Thomas Aquinas, *Summa Theologicae*, Question 83, Article 6.
[5] Romans 5:6.
[6] Ephesians 2:5.

> if some end up in hell for eternity, God is a moral monster. Why? Because he could have saved everyone since salvation is unconditional and not freely chosen. And if God imposes salvation on some without their free assent and cooperation, then the love they have for God is not genuine and God can take no real delight in it. Love that is not freely given is not real love.[7]

The last sentence of Olson's observation is central to his argument, and ultimately to his Arminianism: love that is not freely given is not real love. In this system, it is assumed that God must be a moral monster if He imposes guilt or salvation without humans having the freedom to willingly make choices leading to either. Further, the love He demands can never be real love, because it is not authenticated by choice.

These are sweeping statements with broad implications. True justice requires choice. Moral responsibility requires choice. Authentic love requires choice. If these statements are correct, then one has no choice but to admit the centrality of choice and, ultimately, free choice. At first glance, these three assertions seem viable – perhaps even necessary, but they are actually subject to fatal (in my estimation) flaws.

First, they are self-authenticated and are not exegetically defensible. In Scripture, love is commanded. Even if we have the choice not to comply, what kind of love is demanded? Might someone argue that if love is mandated it cannot be authentic? In 1 John 4:11, we are told that "…if God so loved us, we ought to love one another." We are morally obligated because of His actions to take actions of our own. Peter takes things even a step further. He notes that "like the Holy One who called you, be holy

---

[7] Roger Olson, "An Arminian Account of Free Will," at Catalyst, April 1, 2012, viewed at http://www.catalystresources.org/an-arminian-account-of-free-will/.

in all your behavior."[8] In this case we are obligated to holiness not by God's actions but by His character. And while the imperative is passive (*genethete* is aorist passive imperative, to be exact), it still reflects at least a mandated submission to becoming holy.

The fact remains that both Peter and John recognize we are morally obligated without any choice in being so. Paul informs us that we have been chosen to be in Him before the world was even founded.[9] Not only do we *not have a choice* in this matter, but He takes that choice for Himself. And again, the Father "predestined us to adoption as sons through Jesus Christ to Himself, according to the kind intention of His will..."[10]

It is God's will that is intentional and activated here, not ours. Regardless of whether this is a result of foreknowledge (as some might argue from the order of Rom 8:29), God is still making determinations before we have the opportunity to act. Even if His action is based simply on His foreknowledge, once He predestines and chooses, the outcome is assured. Where does human volition fit into that equation? The only time Paul addresses that question directly is in Romans 9:16, 19-20 when he reasons, "So then it does not depend on the man who runs or the man who wills, but on God who has mercy...You will say to me then, 'why does He still find fault, for who resists His will?' On the contrary, who are you, O man, who answers back to God? The thing molded will not say to the molder 'Why did you make me like this?' will it?"

These Biblical writers are univocal in their claims that in asserting His own sovereignty and choice God is trumping

---

[8] 1 Peter 1:16.
[9] Ephesians 1:4.
[10] 1:5.

human volition at the very outset. Consequently, Scripture itself does not support the idea that human moral responsibility requires human choice. It is worth noting that this does not mean that there is no human choice in any context, there certainly is, but is that choice autonomous or free? Augustine's comment is helpful:

> It is not the case, therefore, that because God foreknew what would be in the power of our wills, there is for that reason nothing in the power of our wills. For he who foreknew this did not foreknow nothing. Moreover, if He who foreknew what would be in the power of our wills did not foreknow nothing, but something, assuredly, even though He did foreknow, there is something in the power of our wills. Therefore we are by no means compelled, either, retaining the prescience of God, to take away the freedom of the will, or, retaining the freedom of the will, to deny that He is prescient of future things, which is impious. But we embrace both. We faithfully and sincerely confess both. The former, that we may believe well; the latter, that we may live well. For he lives ill who does not believe well concerning God.[11]

As Augustine says, there is indeed power in our wills. Yet we can also say that the power of God's will is decisive – He is sovereign, not us. The point here is not to deny human volition, but to suggest that human volition does not undergird anything. It is a gift that we indeed possess, but it does not govern.

A second flaw with the idea that moral responsibility demands choice is that it is self-contradictory. Clearly we are thrust into moral responsibility without any say in the matter. It makes little sense to argue that our having freedom of volition *after that fact* somehow allows God to maintain His justice. No, it is simpler than that. We have no volitional voice regarding our beginning to exist, where we begin to exist, to whom we are born,

---

[11] Augustine, *City of God*, Chapter 9,93.

and into what moral responsibility we are born. To suggest that *after that point* God must grant us freedom of volition accomplishes nothing in support of the argument that our freedom of volition is necessary. In fact, that suggestion is guilty of claiming one degree of the same quality as acceptable and another degree unacceptable.

The suggestion is self-contradictory, and the implications are significant. If God causes us to exist without our permission, then we are thrust into an existence over which we have no say. If He causes us to be born without our choosing, how could it possibly be wrong for us to commit suicide, if indeed moral responsibility necessitates choice? Under such conditions *suicide would be humanity's first moral right.* And yet I know of no free-will advocate who would laud suicide as morally praiseworthy.

A third flaw with the idea that moral responsibility demands choice is that if true it would eliminate God's freedom as Creator to determine what does and does not constitute warrant for moral responsibility – *unless God created the idea that moral responsibility demands choice.* We have already seen that Scripture advocates the idea that moral responsibility does not demand choice, so it seems untenable that God could be accurately described as having put in place choice as prerequisite to moral responsibility.

Further, if God is bound by a set of rules in this regard, then upon what basis is such regulation grounded? The existence of a separate absolute and higher morality that binds even God would imply that God is not the ultimate Moralist. The assertions that love, moral responsibility, and justice all require choice – these assertions all fall on the horns of the same dilemma: if these are true without God having made them true, then He is subject to them, and He is not the absolute Standard.

If He is not the absolute Standard, then whatever *is* that standard is more worthy of worship than He is. In short, that standard would be the true sovereign, and God would be merely an intermediary. The real question, then, is whether or not He has made the assertions true. Even a cursory examination of Scripture shows that He has not made them true.

23
Is God a Jerk?

Ananias, you sold property to give money to the church. But then you kept some and said you didn't. *Dead.* Sapphira – you did too? *Dead.* Uzzah, you reached out to protect God's ark of the covenant from falling on the ground. *Dead.* Gehazi, you wanted some kickback for God's healing of Naaman? *Leprosy* (painful way of getting dead). Job's sons, just because you are Job's sons – *dead.* Moses, you hit a rock instead of talking to it. *Dead (No Promised Land for you).* Lot's wife, you looked back. How could you??? *Dead* (creatively dead, but not any less dead). David's and Bathsheba's child, you did nothing wrong, but your parents did. *Dead.* Korah, you took some money and a cloak from a dead guy? *Dead.* Korah's family, you have the misfortune of being related to Korah. *Dead.* Christians in Corinth, you aren't doing the Lord's Supper right. *Dead.* And the list goes on.

Satan, you introduced sin to the human race, and caused all manner of pain and suffering. *Dead?* No, you get to hang around for all of human history and cause destruction. Cain, you brutally murdered your own brother. *Dead?* No, you get special protection from God. Canaanites, you were murderous, idolatrous, and generally awful. *Dead?* Nope. You get four hundred more years to be scoundrels, and your children's children's children get to pay the price. David, you committed adultery and murder. *Dead?* Not you. You get to be part of an everlasting kingdom. Paul, you persecuted Jesus and murdered Christians. *Dead?* No, you get to be the most prolific apostle. And this list, also, goes on.

Very simply put, God's morality, as evidenced in these Biblical accounts, does not match ours. Everyone in the first list we would probably let off with a warning and maybe a public apology. Their punishments do not fit the crime, from our perspective. On the other hand, those in the second list we would tar, feather, strangle, and burn. Then we would complain about them on Twitter and Facebook. What is wrong with God? Why can't He get this morality and justice thing right? If you and I approached things the way He appears to at times, we would be considered by our peers to be jerks of the highest order. So it shouldn't be hard to say that from our perspective *God is a jerk*.

But there is a key phrase that we have to consider: *our perspective*. This life is all we know, because it is all we are presently equipped to sense and experience. Consequently, we value our brief life on earth more than anything else. *But God doesn't*. As the Creator, He has perspective that we don't. He knows the rest of the story. Here's one part of that story we often leave out: Jesus, you are God in the flesh, and the perfect model of humanity. There is no other like you, and you are the richest treasure ever to walk the planet. *Dead* (and then alive…mustn't leave out that part, either*)*.

God allowing His own Son to die – the very image, essence, and glory of Himself. To us this makes no sense. Some have even called this divine child abuse, though that accusation is ridiculous, especially considering that Jesus willingly gave His own life.[1] He could have done it differently. He could have done it in so many ways, but for whatever reason, He chose this one. Jesus died to pay a substitutionary death for all,[2] so that all who believe in Him have eternal life.[3] But what about those who don't believe in Him? Jesus made no apology for His assertion that He would, one day, judge, and that those who don't believe will have a resurrection in judgment.[4]

Does God offer mercy to all with the threat of eternal judgment for those who don't believe? *Yes.* What kind of horrible offer is that? How can He say He loved the whole world when most of it (presumably not taking the "narrow way") will be unbelieving and undergo His judgment? From our perspective that might be more madness than love.

And there it is again: *our perspective*. Here we come to the realization that we are in a battle of perspectives. In one corner, you have humanity, blindfolded and impotent. In the other is God, who allegedly created everything. If He is the Creator, then He has sovereign rights over His creation – plus the added bonus of seeing and knowing everything. The bell rings, and the battle of perspectives begins. Who are you going to bet on? We don't even have the capability to understand what love is without Him.

---

[1] John 10:18.
[2] 1 John 2:2.
[3] John 3:16.
[4] John 5:27-29.

"But," one might wonder, "are you saying that might makes right?" "Does this mean that the strongest gets to determine what is correct?" Not exactly. I would say it differently: might doesn't make right, but *absolute might certainly does*. Because only the Creator of all has ultimate might. And does not the one who designed it all have the prerogative to set the rules?

The question is simple. Whose perspective will we trust? He tells us that, "The fear of the Lord is the beginning of all wisdom."[5] He tells us that there is no injustice with Him,[6] and that "I will be gracious to whom I will be gracious, and will show compassion on whom I will show compassion."[7] He tells us that He loved the world and sent His Son to die so that all might have life by believing in His name.[8]

When it comes to morality and justice, the Creator isn't obligated in the same way He obligates His creation. Just as a father has the prerogative to restrict his children from driving a car, all while driving a car himself, the Creator is no hypocrite for operating outside of the standards He requires for His creatures. And we can only understand Him – who He is and what He expects – to the extent He has revealed Himself in His word. Even there He doesn't give us the whole picture, so we have limited information – perhaps just enough to make an informed decision and to have a relationship with Him. We have to decide whose perspective we will trust: our holy and loving Creator's, or our own. If we choose poorly – not relying on His love and grace – then *we are the jerks*, not Him. Don't be a jerk.

---

[5] Proverbs 1:7.
[6] Romans 9:14.
[7] Exodus 33:19.
[8] John 3:16, 20:31.

24

Decisions, Decisions:
The Interplay of Sovereignty and Freedom In Decision Making

How do we know if we are following God's will? Does He sovereignly place guideposts in front of us, and if we miss one, we are out of His will? Does He entrust us with opportunities and simply leave us to do the work? Does He choose certain things for us and if we miss those, then His plan for our life is irrevocably thwarted? How does He intend for us to live – does His sovereignty direct us or are we simply totally free and responsible?

Further, we can ask how God guides us. Does He provide us with mystical Gideon's fleeces at every turn so we might get tangible confirmations that we are on the right path? Or should we anticipate that the choices we are making are to be assessed in light of Biblical principles, and the specifics are matters of freedom? Is there one way to fulfill a task that God intends for us to complete or are there multiple ways we might be successful? Does choosing one vocation over another mean we might miss the will of God? Or one mate, or one path in life versus another? The passages and principles considered in the preceding chapters are foundational to answering these important and practical questions. Just as the answer in previous chapters has been neither door number one nor door number two, the answers are not as clear cut as choosing between two opposite options.

On the one hand, we might look at obstacles in our path and perceive that God is shutting doors and trying to direct us to a different path. On the other, we can recognize that there are adversaries (like Satan) who would seek to make our journey more difficult, so that we will change direction rather than staying the course. Herein lies the problem: How can we *know* when God is blocking the path and wants us off it, and when adversaries are blocking the path and want us off it? The short answer is that we *can't*. We don't have a "hermeneutic" for such things, and so we must simply rely on understanding God's character, how He has revealed Himself, and what He has revealed about what He expects us to do.

For example, He has told us to pray without ceasing and to be always thankful.[1] He has told us to trust in Him, delight in Him, and commit our way to Him.[2] We understand we are to be singularly focused on Him.[3] Yet, He has not told us who we should marry, though He has provided extensive guidelines for us regarding how we should make that choice. He has not told us what job we should do, though He has given us much instruction regarding how we should use our time and how we should prioritize. He has not told us that we are to diagnose difficult circumstances as His redirecting efforts. So rather than

---

[1] 1 Thessalonians 5:16-17.
[2] Psalm 37:3-5.
[3] Matthew 6:33.

trying to read circumstances as if they were tea leaves or as if they were the stars of the zodiac, perhaps we should simply recognize that even within His sovereign control He has given us choices, He provides us with very specific direction regarding how we should make those choices, but then He leaves the choices up to us – even while exerting His sovereignty in our lives.

A property owner was about to leave for his journey, but before he departed, he invested three stewards with the task of increasing his resources. He gave each an amount appropriate for his ability, and then went on his way. Two of the three were faithful, providing a 100% return on their investments, while the other was so fearful of losing what was entrusted, that he didn't risk what was given to him.[4] This parable illustrates the importance of good stewardship, of making the most of the opportunity provided, and of being prepared for inevitable accountability. The parable also illustrates another important principle. The property owner left the investments to the stewards and left. His design wasn't to direct their decisions, but to allow them the latitude to make their decisions, for better or for worse.

So then, was the outcome of this investing simply the result of the stewards' *efforts*? On the contrary, we plant, we water, but God causes the growth.[5] As it is said elsewhere, unless the Lord builds the house he that builds labors in vain.[6] God controls outcomes to the degree He wants to. He can choose to bless efforts or not, and He has the prerogative to bless good or bad efforts if He chooses. Moses seems to recognize this when

---

[4] Matthew 25:14-30.
[5] 1 Corinthians 3:6-8.
[6] Psalm 127:1.

he asks God to confirm the work of his hands.[7] Moses understands that if God blesses, the work will be blessed, and if not, it won't.

Solomon asserts that "the mind of man plans his way, but the Lord directs his steps."[8] This is not an indicator of God's constant tangible intervention. Remember, He already holds all things together,[9] He doesn't need to intervene. Consequently, if we are looking for tangible ways to confirm His will beyond that which He has specifically revealed, then we are left with unverifiable speculations, and we are faced with the dilemma of trying to interpret which are godly obstacles and which are of Satan. For example, Paul diagnoses that there is a wide door of service opened up to him, and there are many adversaries.[10] He was convinced that he was going the right direction because he was fulfilling the broad task God had given him, making the most of every opportunity. Further, he could recognize that those who opposed that stewardship were indeed adversaries.

It is worth noting that even though God was gracious to Gideon in providing him a sign so that Gideon would have confidence he was making the right decision, Gideon recognized that he was asking God for something that was not in accordance with trust. When Gideon makes his request, he adds, "Do not let your anger burn against me that I may speak once more..."[11] Gideon was not relying on what God had already told him, and was instead seeking further confirmation. It is remarkable that God was patient with Gideon in this, and while He provided the

---

[7] Psalm 90:17.
[8] Proverbs 16:12.
[9] Colossians 1:17.
[10] 1 Corinthians 16:9.
[11] Judges 6:39.

requested sign for Gideon, He makes no commitment to provide signs like that for us. Much like Jesus allowed Thomas to see and touch His scars so that Thomas would believe, still Jesus said, "Because you have seen Me, have you believed? Blessed are they who have not seen and believed."[12] God understands our weakness of faith and He is gracious in how He treats us. He also wants us to grow in our faith, simply relying on Him and His word.

Peter was actually walking on water, being focused on Jesus. But the moment he began to focus on the storm around him, he began to sink.[13] It is fitting then that Peter would later write to believers who were enduring hardship, encouraging them to focus on Him, on what He had told them, and on what He had done for them. Nowhere in Peter's letters does he pray for changed circumstances, he simply challenges believers to endure and rejoice in difficulty.

Sometimes we speak of what God has called us to do. We speak of God calling us to vocations or to ministries or to locations or to actions. Unfortunately, we can get very theologically sloppy in doing so. Never do we see God calling church-age believers to any of these things (though Jesus did formally call His apostles). We are called according to His purpose,[14] to His kingdom in glory,[15] and even called for suffering.[16] But when we are looking for some experiential calling, we find ourselves in a sea of subjectivity that cannot provide certainty and is not verifiable. We are looking for

---

[12] John 20:29.
[13] Matthew 14:28-31.
[14] Romans 8:28.
[15] 1 Thessalonians 2:12.
[16] 1 Peter 2:21.

tangible expressions of His sovereignty, when He is instead providing us with stewardships and asking us to plant and water as He has equipped us.

Now, this is not to say that God is not actively involved in our lives, even as we are making choices. The principle of His sovereignty does not go away simply because we may be fulfilling our responsibility. Recall that Romans 9:16 does acknowledge that man is running and willing, but the outcomes (particularly in that context, the application of mercy) belong to God. In His grace, God has provided for us the perfect interface between His sovereignty and our accountability. In the midst of difficulty, if we are uncertain, we can ask Him for wisdom, and He commits to providing it.[17] He does not tell us to ask Him for signs, but rather to seek His wisdom. So, rather than constantly evaluating circumstances as a litmus test for whether or not we are going the right direction, if we keep focused on Him and on what He has said in His word, then we will be going the right way. In so doing, we can have certainty regardless of how tumultuous our circumstances. He is sovereign and in control. In that He has provided us a dual-faceted mechanism for good stewardship of every resource and opportunity: *faith and obedience*. If we are trusting in Him, and walking in what He has revealed we will have confidence in His direction for our lives. If on the other hand, we are constantly asking Him for new revelation in or through our circumstances, that shows that we are not paying enough attention to what He has already told us, and we miss out on the confidence and joy He has sovereignly embedded into our lives through freedom.

---

[17] James 1:5.

25
The Sofa Rule

Once upon a time there was a woman and a man
Who loved each other so much – as much as anyone can.
They courted and married, and soon they had daughters –
The kind that bring joy to their mothers and fathers.

These daughters were like their mother in more ways than one,
They were godly, and pretty, with smiles like the sun.
To them many gifts our Father had given,
And they grew to become remarkable young women.

One day, when the daughters were still little girls,
Their parents bought a sofa – the best for their little world.
They could all sit together and enjoy each other.
There was room for the girls, for their father and mother.

The Sofa Rule

The sofa was a velvety dark kind of brown,
And it was so very soft for them all to sit down.
Except for being a bit lumpy in a few little places,
It put smiles on the whole family's faces.

Some time passed, and the family enjoyed the seat,
But the parents began to notice that it was not kept so neat.
Crumbs and spilled food showed up all around
Even though the sofa was an especially dark brown,

After all, you can see many things on furniture that shade
So the nice, new look, quickly began to fade.
To be sure that the couch wasn't completely defiled,
The parents made a rule for the daughters, and just for a while.

They needed to obey, and the parents explained how:
The daughters couldn't eat on the sofa – but only for now.
They could eat at the table, or even sitting on the floor.
They could eat in the kitchen, or leaning against a door.

But the sofa was off limits as an eating tool,
The daughters paid attention to *the sofa rule*.
They received the direction without any complaints,
And followed it faithfully, like angels or saints.

As time passed, though, these daughters began to wonder,
As they saw their parents eating, not under
Not beside, or next to, and not even over –
The parents were eating *right on the sofa*!

Again, the daughters did not complain,
And to that point they had been faithful to refrain,
But one of them couldn't help but to ask,
"Why do *you* break the rule...why is it just our task?"

Were their parents somehow immune?
Was their behavior truly out of tune?
It was a completely reasonable question, for sure.
(They asked lots of good questions, with hearts that were pure.)

After all, the rule was etched in stone
(even the KJV version of the rule was well known):
"thou shalt not eat food upon the sofa...
No food, nor drinks...nor bubbling soda."

As the daughters' level of concern grew and grew,
they began to reason to themselves that this couldn't be true.
For they were certain their parents loved them a lot,
But they wondered if their parents had just been caught.

Daddy smiled gently as Daddies often do,
And sat with them, explaining a thing both important and true.
"You must understand something, Lovelies," he began to share,
"Your mother and I love you far beyond compare,

And sometimes we need to set boundaries to guide
For blessings to guard and wisdom to provide.
See, right now you are just learning to eat and not make a mess
– but sometimes, you don't quite pass the test.

The Sofa Rule

Still, we are patient with you and give you freedom to grow;
Sometimes part of that means we are wise to say 'no'."
The daughters realized right then and there,
That the rule wasn't unjust and it wasn't unfair.

It wasn't designed to make their lives sad,
But to give them freedom, and to make their heart glad.
The limits were good, they weren't bad in the least.
They were just what was needed to help them know peace.

But Daddy had more still yet to say,
The daughters were listening, as Mommy smiled not far away.
"There is another thing about this sofa rule –
it isn't the law, it's more like a tool.

It was designed not for your Mother and not for me,
but for you two – listen carefully and you will see!
We gave you this rule to help guide your behavior.
In this rule we are trying to model our Savior.

You are learning how to have a sofa and keep it in good shape.
Your Mommy and I already know how to behave.
So when we eat on the sofa we do it with care
Not to spill crumbs and food over here and over there.

See, *you* need the rule, not Mommy or me,
As you learn the truth, you learn how to be free.
And it is our job to guide you and to help you to grow.
I am glad you asked, and am thankful that now you know."

"But Daddy, how can there be a rule *you* don't have to follow?
Doesn't that make the rule kind of hollow?"
"Aren't you doing wrong when you eat where we can't?
Aren't you sinning when you eat where we shan't?"

"Another good question," said Mommy, with not even a sigh,
"We are so glad you want to understand *why*.
The sofa is ours, so we must decide
It's not about us, nor a matter of pride,

We must be wise with all that God has entrusted
Because it is all His – *He* has invested.
And because you are our daughters – entrusted by God, too,
We want to help you grow, we desire that for you."

So, the daughters learned a valuable lesson that day –
That even helped them understand God in a significant way.
They lived happily ever after with peace and rejoicing,
Knowing that God had a plan in His brilliant appointing.

You see, God has His own sofa rule of sorts –
More than one, actually, as some will report.
He is the Creator and Owner of all that there is,
And it is His place to govern and make sure nothing is amiss.

His rules we follow and ought to recognize,
That He's made them for His own glory and to help sanctify us.
We benefit from knowing that what He has designed is good,
And it is God who determines how we can live like we should.

His holiness isn't subject to our kind of limit,
And all that He does comes from within it.
Even though sometimes we may not like them so much,
His rules benefit us and show His caring touch.

We should always remember He's not bound by these rules,
He fashioned and designed them to be His own tools.
They teach us about truth, about love, about grace,
And they help us to get a glimpse of His wonderful face.

One day in heaven, when before Him we stand,
I think we will finally realize His plan.
Of course, we won't figure out all that He has done,
But we will learn and discover – that is the very best kind of fun.

In the meantime, we journey with limited perspective,
But we can trust Him and do the work of detectives.
He's given us wisdom, truth, and the way,
To be close to Him – walking as His children every day.

He saved us from sin by the blood of His Son,
He simply asked us to believe in Him and know He's the One.
He invites us to come and to reason together,
To learn and discover how His way is better.

He governs all nature and everything in it,
And He has plans to redeem, to complete, and to finish.
We are detectives in life – all of us are,
As we investigate God's wonder, even if from afar.

The Sofa Rule

God is the Creator and He makes the rules,
So let us not live as arrogant fools,
Who think that our morality is greater than His,
And that He must submit to our own thoughts and whims.

God has a sofa, I suppose you could say,
And on that sofa He lets us sit and play.
But He governs that sofa, as the sovereign King,
And it is His own sofa – it is not our thing.

So, reader, be wise, don't think like a fool,
God has the right to make His own sofa rule.

www.ingramcontent.com/pod-product-compliance
Lightning Source LLC
Chambersburg PA
CBHW022112040426
42450CB00006B/667